GREEN LIVING IN THE URBAN JUNGLE

GREEN LIVING
in the
URBAN JUNGLE

Lucy Siegle

with original photography by Duncan Soar

 Green Books

First published in 2001
by Green Books Ltd
Foxhole, Dartington
Totnes, Devon TQ9 6EB

Design by Rick Lawrence
Tel: 01803 840956

Text printed by Bell & Bain Ltd, Glasgow

British Library Cataloguing in Publication Data
available on request

ISBN 1 903998 04 2

Contents

Contents (continued)

Acknowledgements

When I started my green experiment, I naïvely thought it would be breeze. Consequently, lots of people need to be thanked for bailing me out with their advice, support and enthusiasm. Top of the list is Ben, who deserves much praise for accompanying me on my eco-experiment, for enjoying it, and for being photographed riding the electric trike in heavy traffic. Other members of the large supporting cast include my mum, Claire Meharg, for all her good ideas and unstinting enthusiasm, Duncan Soar for taking great pictures at horribly early hours of the morning, John Elford at Green Books for his calmness, knowledge and infinite patience, and Rick Lawrence for his inspired design.

I would like to say a big thank you to everyone who has contributed to this book by giving up precious time to tell me about their green leanings, lifestyles and projects; to everyone who magnanimously agreed to be photographed—especially some of the more camera-shy. And finally, thanks to all the original greenies who have entered into the light-hearted approach, without even raising their eyebrows at references to turnip-huggers. After all, they are safe in the knowledge that they set the wheels in motion many years ago.

Chapter 1

absolute
beginners

This is a handbook for urbanites everywhere who have lost touch with their green roots, and want to reclaim them with the minimum of fuss and maximum of benefits. Whether you live in a small town, suburban area or fully-fledged metropolis, it isn't easy to escape from a synthetic lifestyle where nature becomes increasingly redundant. Away from inspiring pastoral scenes, reminders of Mother Nature are few and far between.

Some of us seem naturally predisposed to the metropolitan way of life. We enjoy the fast pace, the convenience and stimulation of having everything from clubs to art galleries on our doorstep. Then of course there are the people who were born and bred in an urban environment and have never felt the need to leave. But just because we have chosen these aspects of urban life, why should we have to compromise our health, environment and principles? And if this seems like we want to have our organic cake and eat it, well—why not? Just because we choose to live in the big smoke, it shouldn't necessarily follow that we should also have to choke on it.

REALITY V DREAMWORLD

Despite our preference for urban life, there is no denying that the daily grind can get to us in a big way. Your average urbanite with green aspirations will be used to hatching plans to leave all the chaotic madness behind. Stuck on a train, in a traffic jam or perhaps during the scrum of Christmas shopping, you drift off into a reverie where you bolt to a small-holding on an island off the west coast of Scotland. Shunning supermarkets and 24-hour petrol stations in favour of getting back to nature, you imagine a seductive subsistence existence, living off the fat of the land,

A familiar sight: approaching urban consumer meltdown.

tending a few sheep and breathing invigorating fresh air. At some point however, you will crash back to earth. If Foot and Mouth and BSE have shown us anything, it is that rural life can be far from the cosy, stress-free idyll of contemporary folklore. Couple that stark reality with the prospect of being stranded without our creature comforts, and the proposition looks less attractive.

Well, this is where this handbook comes in! Once we have decided that we prefer our vistas to be of the urban variety, we need to set about eliminating some of the negative aspects of our urban lifestyle. In this way we can stop compromising our health, general wellbeing and principles, and consequently some of the stresses traditionally associated with an urban existence. We're not going to create an instant utopia, but by adopting a greener outlook we can reduce some of the personal and environmental stresses that we experience and create. You may have green aspirations already—perhaps you could be termed light green—or maybe this an entirely new venture. Whatever the case, this book is dedicated to help you make sustainable changes in a rational, graduated and easy way.

ERASING FOOTPRINTS

If you've heard people going on about ecological footprints, you may have wondered exactly what they were talking about. It is basically a way of explaining the impression we are leaving on the planet—how much of an indelible mark we are making. In cities, we're each making less of a mark and more of a crater. Take London: each of the capital's three million households needs the equivalent of 18 acres to support it, generates around 22 kg of rubbish, emits around six tonnes of carbon dioxide per year, and uses 165 litres of water a day. Other major cities follow closely behind. It's not rocket science to realize that unless we reverse this, we (and future generations) are in big trouble. In urban environments we need to act now to decrease our so-called 'ecological footprint'.

John strikes a pose outside the Organic Bus Stop—a veritable Aladdin's cave of organic items, as well as offering a refill service for Ecover cleaning products.

WHY GREEN IS GOOD

The idea that 'green is good' is obviously not a new one. Besides decreasing our ecological footprints, we need to take care of our own health. Common sense tells us that living a more natural lifestyle is better for us, more in harmony with the natural world and natural cycles, and protects the environment. Recent food scares have emphasized the problems we now experience as the food that we eat has become so far removed from natural farming practices. Everything from rearing animals to the packaging and processing of food has come under scrutiny. The end result is that we are now demanding unadulterated products, with a clear journey from the field to the table. 'Organic' has become a buzzword as we try to rediscover fresh food that has more in common with nature than with manufacturing. If we can't have all-organic products, we at least want them to be green: made with due respect to the environment and as free as possible from additives.

GREEN IMAGE

There has never been a better or easier time to adopt a green lifestyle. A proliferation of businesses dedicated to providing green and organic products, services and advice means that finding alternatives and implementing changes has never been more simple.

It hasn't always been this way of course. In the past green concerns were associated with tree-huggers, kaftan wearers, mung beans and tie-dye, and any leanings towards eco-friendly living meant that you would probably be ostracized by your neighbours. But nowadays you couldn't be in more salubrious company, as the great and the good rush to embrace green living. Mini panics from food scares, transport dilemmas and health scares have all helped to convince us that we should focus our attention on living more harmoniously with the natural world.

STRESS-FREE CHANGES

Let's face it: the last thing we frazzled urbanites need is more stress. As it is, the majority of us spend a large proportion of our lives racing round and trying to cram everything in. Consequently we tend to steer clear of lifestyle changes: we can't accommodate disruption, or devote any more time to the basic routines of daily life. Luckily, by sourcing green and organic products and services, implementing simple systems and planning ahead, we can negate any inconvenience and minimize any disruption. Simplicity really is the key here, whether it's a matter of setting up an effective recycling system, cutting down on waste and packaging, or planning a shopping trip. Adhering to a simple 'less is more' policy will cut down on unnecessary stuff, and lessen the stress that clutter leads to. It's also about replacing the old with the new, and where to find comparable alternatives.

AVOIDING ORGANIC PANIC!

Crises in farming, food scares, GM food, chemical reactions, increased allergies—all of these headline-grabbing concerns are enough to cause the most rational of persons to don a space suit and eat only raw vegetables. Such crises have managed to shake up our organic sensibilities, but we need to translate this into meaningful changes that will gradually enhance our lives and become part of a workable long-term plan.

You have a great opportunity to shake up your urban existence: there's a host of resources, services and opportunities that weren't around before. Old habits don't have to die hard, especially when replaced with new improved ones!

WORKING THE HANDBOOK

You can be as flexible you like when using this book. If you hate reading instructions and prefer to jump in at the deep end (possibly returning sheepishly to the instructions later on), you could well have skipped this part already. Read the Top Tips in each chapter and use the chapter headings as a guide to some of the changes you can begin to implement. If you prefer a more systematic approach, you can read through each section covering the major aspects of an urban lifestyle and work through the changes and initiatives. Or if you believe in learning through trial and error, you'll appreciate the diary sections, where a great deal of both trial and error has been done for you. Information and facts are mixed in with theory and practice in each section (you can use them to evangelize to your friends, as ammunition in arguments, or even to persuade yourself if necessary). For extra inspiration, the mini guides and profiles give you the chance to read about some successful working projects in cities around the UK. At the end of the book you'll find a round-up, and a mini directory of organizations, should you want to take things further.

TOP TIPS ON GETTING STARTED

The good news is that, to implement green changes, you don't suddenly have to start keeping pigs in your back garden and wearing hemp smocks. Nor do you have to abandon all of your consumerist instincts—in fact the skills you have built up as a dedicated shopper will help you no end in order to search out the best green products.

Discover the potential of your own living space. Start to think where you could put recycling bins, leave a bicycle and grow some potted herbs. However spatially challenged your environment may be, there are bound to be some opportunities.

As the old adage puts it, 'Rome wasn't built in a day', and nor will your green utopia. Remember that we want graceful, constructive changes, not organic panic leading to a buying frenzy. Start to implement changes by beginning to shop for green alternatives to core products that you use, such as tins and jars of food, low energy light bulbs and recycled paper. This way you will slowly stock up on the basic products rather than bankrupting yourself by hastily using up or throwing out all non-green and non-organic items, and replacing them all in one fell swoop.

Start to look for alternatives—not just for food and drink items, but also other products such as cosmetics, washing powders, cleaning liquids, toiletries and even pet food (if you want to extend your green sensibilities to your dog or cat). As you read through this book you'll come across more and more ideas about where to find good alternatives.

Get information from your council. Arm yourself with council leaflets (often available from the library) or look on the net to see what help you are entitled to from your council. Many run comprehensive domestic recycling schemes, but you may have to request the service from them.

There is information everywhere on green services and products. The more businesses that spring up, the more information that appears. Keep leaflets together in a folder or on a pin board. The net is an invaluable source of information, and it is a good idea to invest in a comprehensive directory: try *The Organic Directory* edited by Clive Litchfield, so that you are aware of a wealth of options. You can also find it online, at <www.theorganicdirectory.co.uk>.

Ask questions in specialist shops and markets, and even contact mail order and internet services to find out exactly what they're offering and how they differ from conventional products and services. Swot up on labels (see Chapter 2, Go Wild With Food), but don't be afraid to ask about the validity of any green or organic claims. Remember: bona fide, accredited stall holders will generally be happy to share their knowledge, and should show their accreditation certificates on request.

diary: humble beginnings

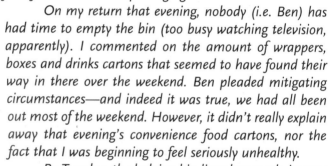

Lucy (the author) lives with her husband Ben in a shoebox-sized flat in South London. In common with many other urban dwellings, there are no spare rooms or storage space and a small balcony provides the only exterior space. This is a real life account of their first steps in going green. . . .

Does anyone enjoy Monday mornings? Certainly not me, as I follow my usual pattern of staggering into our kitchen and desperately try to locate my house keys before sprinting to catch the train (fortunately, it's usually delayed). My mission to find my keys is hampered by running straight into our overflowing rubbish bin. Even though there's only two of us, we do seem to produce a remarkable amount of trash at the weekends, and our Monday morning bin is overflowing with junk food cartons and packaging.

On my return that evening, nobody (i.e. Ben) has had time to empty the bin (too busy watching television, apparently). I commented on the amount of wrappers, boxes and drinks cartons that seemed to have found their way in there over the weekend. Ben pleaded mitigating circumstances—and indeed it was true, we had all been out most of the weekend. However, it didn't really explain away that evening's convenience food cartons, nor the fact that I was beginning to feel seriously unhealthy.

By Tuesday, the bulging bin-liner has made its way downstairs to the communal rubbish bins, courtesy of Ben. He also spotted a green box with a couple of wine bottles, which had been brought out by one of our neighbours. We have a large collection of bottles ourselves which sit underneath the kitchen counter awaiting their final destination, so this struck us a useful idea. Ben resolved to phone the council or ask the neighbours about the recycling system.

Later that week a newspaper article caught my attention. It featured the foods that my household likes to stock up on a weekly basis: full of additives, preservatives, emulsifiers and all kinds of potions. Apparently one apple can be subjected to sixty artificial chemicals, and the really bad news is that we just don't know what these do to us. Ben also made progress with the recycling box: he emailed Lambeth Council to order a green box from them. The email was acknowledged, and a box will be delivered in a week. Hey presto! Our eco-awakening seems to have finally happened. I even bought a box of energy-saving light bulbs. A small gesture, but it all helps!

Over the weekend we discuss our green changes. We don't have much to be smug about yet, but Ben and I are convinced we should build on these

diary

very humble foundations as a kind of social experiment to see how green even we can become. I dedicate Sunday afternoon to surfing the net to get some other ideas. The Soil Association website (<www.soilassociation.org>), which I had seen mentioned in an article, is my first port of call. This site, recently restructured, is packed full of information and advice on organic produce, tips and initiatives. There are also plenty of links to other green-related sites. All that remains for us to do now is to act on the advice!

focus on cardiff

(An interview with Steve Garrett, Cultural Concerns)

The Riverside area in Cardiff has suffered from something of an image problem. Close to the centre of the Welsh capital, it had traditionally been one of the poorest areas in Cardiff, with many families on low incomes and with high rates of unemployment. However, despite visitors to Cardiff generally giving the area a wide berth, many residents were keen to show how much the community had changed in recent years.

The whole project began when we got the annual Riverside festival going again, which coincided with a programme of urban renewal which had given the whole area a facelift. This event helped to get rid of some of the preconceptions people had about Riverside, and reinforced the fact that the area had a strong, special identity. In fact it made me realize that food and music could actually have a more positive effect on the community than an urban renewal grant!

Once the festival was a success, we turned our attention to establishing a more consistent project in the area. We realized that there were a few corner shops, but nowhere in Riverside that sold fresh food. A lot of people in the community, especially if they are on low incomes, don't

photo by Steve Garrett, Cultural Concerns

have a car, and don't fancy dragging a couple of kids around in the rain. They can't get to the nearest supermarket because it's not close enough. So we decided to try out a food market, using local producers and selling fresh food. At first the market was set up under the umbrella of the festival, and a series of summer food fairs were held in the park. These progressed to a couple of Christmas fairs. The idea was to get local people trading, and to make fresh local food available to local people in their own backyard.

We were keen to push the sense that it was a community market and that we were selling local, Welsh and organic food. The real challenge was to make the market inclusive enough to attract the diverse, multicultural population of Riverside to buy. We were anxious not to scare people off by promoting 'organic' food which they might immediately associate with expense. It took longer than we expected to attract the minority communities to the market, because at first we attracted a lot of wealthier people from outside the community. However, this was also positive as it helped to prove to everybody that the area had changed.

We did a couple more years in the park as the Riverside Community Market Association, but were keen to move to somewhere that was even more accessible. Last year, we got lucky. We had always wanted the market to run alongside the river Taff, as it seems such a natural space for people to browse and buy local food. When Cardiff stadium was redeveloped, the Council widened the pavement by the river, making it big enough for a riverside market. We then began our pitch with the Council, and called a meeting of the local residents. We finally got permission, and also a grant from The Prince's Trust and Environment Wales.

Whereas before we had rented a marquee for the market, which had proved to be expensive, the grant enabled us to buy our own big canopies, and we began running 18–20 stalls on the first Sunday of every month.

We are now called the Riverside Food Market, which we chose in preference to 'farmers' market' as we wanted to make sure we gave everyone in the community a chance to sell food: alongside Welsh producers there is a local Indian woman who sells samosas, and a lady from Kuwait selling Middle Eastern food. There is a shortage of some producers, but as more and more food markets take off, small producers will again become viable.

The market is going from strength to strength, with a good variety of local producers selling products that they have grown or made themselves. The redevelopment of Cardiff Bay has also opened up the possibility of river taxis operating between the Bay and Riverside. If and when this happens, we hope that day trippers will make Riverside market their first port of call and come and pick up some authentic, fresh food.

urban organics

As well as having a name that any cartoon character would envy, Splott in Cardiff is an area of the city that is on the up and houses the superb Urban Organics store, one of Riverside Market's most enthusiastic stall-holders. The store opened last year to accommodate the business's bur-geoning box scheme and to give owner, Mags Williams, the opportunity to supply a full range of organic produce and sustainable lifestyle prod-ucts to the local and surrounding communities.

Urban Organics came into being when the Williams family tired of supermarkets, and found themselves on a permanent quest for fresh organic produce. Once they had found relatively local suppliers, they became laden down with organic goods for friends and neighbours who began to give them shopping lists. The Urban Organics box scheme was in many ways the next logical step, and the initial scheme soon extended to a 20-mile radius.

These days, the shop is very much part of the Splott community, offering a viable alternative to the anonymity of supermarket shopping. It offers a large range of both essentials and goodies, but one of the high-lights must surely be the bread baked by Alan Davies of The Authentic Bread Company, which comes from relatively nearby, in Gloucestershire. The business also has strong links with producers and suppliers in Wales, meaning that most seasonal fruit and vegetables comes directly from nearby Pencoed, Whitebrook and Medhope.

<www.urbanorganics.co.uk>. Tel: 029 2040 3399, Fax: 029 2025 8032.

Chapter 2

go wild
with food

For most busy urbanites it is enough of a challenge just to muster up enough energy to stagger round the supermarket or local shop at the end of the day. Here we join the other drones in a march around the aisles looking for something vaguely tasty for tea.

Ben and I like food, and consider it to be an essential part of our existence, but we've become increasingly used to ignoring its significance as other aspects of our frantic lives take over. The idea that 'you are what you eat' is hardly a new one—in fact it's a slogan that's done the rounds for years, applied to everything from low fat margarines to the benefits of brown bread. And now, following food scares which have highlighted the problems and limitations of intensive farming, the idea that what you consume has a great bearing on your overall health has become extremely high-profile again.

WHY CONVENTIONAL FOOD
ISN'T MAKING THE GRADE

As metropolitan consumers we don't don green wellies very often, but we can't have failed to notice the problems caused by intensive agricultural practices: we've seen everything from butter mountains and milk lakes, to BSE caused by conventional farming methods. Alongside this, we've seen natural products adulterated by pesticides and preservatives until they have more in common with supplies given to astronauts than fresh food from the ground. Not surprisingly, we are beginning to rebel against this by putting increasing emphasis on natural, fresh food. If a

---

Switching on to fresh, local, greener produce will not only wake up your taste buds and broaden your culinary horizons, but help you cut the umbilical cord to the boring old supermarket and free you from the nightly zombie-style march down the aisles.

combination of lack of energy, lack of time, lack of creative ideas and lack of viable and healthy alternatives have scared us off from changing our eating habits in the past, things look set to change. By the year 2005, the UK is set to become Europe's biggest spender on organic food.

CRAZY FOR ORGANICS

Greener food is the answer to avoiding the chemicals and man-made interference inherent in conventionally grown produce. It is also an essential part of the green experience. When we say green in this context, we are not just talking about apples, cucumbers, lettuce and anything else of a verdant hue, but produce that is grown in harmony with nature and with regard for the environment, without artificial fertilizers, herbicides or pesticides, and as fresh and unadulterated as possible. Organic food is grown to these specifications, and offers us the perfect solution if we want to eat a healthy, environmentally sound diet.

The science behind organic farming is surprisingly simple. As it involves getting rid of the chemicals and much of the man-made interference involved in conventional farming, it is really a case of 'less is more'. It's essentially a low input, low output system, one which our ancestors would have been broadly familiar with. A kind of back-to-basics farming, it focuses on maintaining a sound, healthy, well balanced soil in harmony with nature, using natural composts and fertilizers. Rather than squeezing the land dry, as with conventional farming, crop rotation is an important part of the organic process, resting fields and alternating crops to support the natural ecosystem. If all this talk of soil, yields and crops makes you feel you'd like to be closer to the action, you can always join the International WWOOF Association and spend some real time on an organic farm as a volunteer (see Mini Directory).

Certified organic food means that even though we do our shopping in towns and cities, we can still be sure that what we buy is from the purest possible sources. If something is certified to be organic (check out the symbols and codes below) you can be sure that it has been grown to strict organic standards. Chemical interference is prohibited, and the organic system promotes biodiversity, biological cycles and biological activity in the soil. If it sounds impressive, it's because it is! Without even so much as grabbing a pitchfork, even the most urbane of us city slickers can make a point by supporting sustainable and accountable farming.

ORGANIC CREDENTIALS

Biodynamic farming follows organic principles—and then some. Introduced into the public domain by Rudolph Steiner in 1924, the approach is holistic, working with the forces in nature and treating the whole earth as a living organism. Each farm is considered to be unique. On a biodynamic farm, everything is included in their overall conception of growth and influences: the soil, rocks, the atmosphere, flowers and plants, the seasons and even the rhythms of the planets.

Teresa gets to grips with the juicer.

TOP TEN REASONS FOR PREFERRING ORGANIC

If you are still unconvinced, here are ten very good reasons for changing your shopping basket to an organic one:

1. Eliminate nasty chemicals

Check out the labels on all produce so that you can buy certified organic food where possible (see Label Queen below for tips). This will ensure you are eating fresh, natural food that has not been covered in chemicals. It's a sobering thought that your average innocuous-looking apple has probably been treated with around twenty chemicals, and possibly up to sixty! Some of these won't be removed by rinsing, and peeling the skin won't get rid of the chemicals that have been absorbed. Buying organic will guarantee that your apple is free from these synthetic potions.

2. Increase your vitamin count by eating fresh produce

We're always hearing about how we should eat more fruit and vegetables. We know vitamins, minerals and enzymes are beneficial to our health, but even if we have a pretty varied diet we can still fail to ingest enough of them. This is due to the poor quality of conventionally farmed produce. Fresh, organic produce contains up to 50% more vitamins, minerals and enzymes than intensively farmed produce. Research by the Soil Association has found that organic crops are not only higher in vitamin C and essential minerals but also higher in phytonutrients, which can be beneficial in the treatment of cancer and help to protect plants from pests and disease.

An alternative to sliced white: an artisan bread producer in Borough Market.

3. Boycott Genetically Modified foods
The high profile GM food debate seems set to run and run. The UK public and a good few health and food safety professionals remain unconvinced that genetically modified foods are a good idea. This would seem to be a prudent stance, given that despite substantial industry research no GM companies have been able to find any compelling evidence that GM crops are safe. Looking at the wider picture, it is interesting to note that farmers will not be able to plant seeds from their GM crops, but will need to purchase new seed every year from the GM corporations. Small wonder that farmers in developing countries are protesting against the introduction of GM crops as if their lives depended on it—they do. Fortunately we can use our purchasing power and register our mistrust by buying organic.

4. Give dairy and meat products from conventionally farmed animals a miss
The BSE and Foot and Mouth crises illustrated the very real problems and expedient nature of conventional intensive farming. Conventionally farmed animals are routinely fed antibiotics and hormones, which then enter the food chain. By going for organic alternatives you will not only avoid eating products from adulterated food chains, but also help to address animal welfare.

5. Trust your taste buds
It's really no surprise that organic produce tastes more alive and fresh—that's what it is! Your taste buds will be the first thing to convert, and you'll find it difficult to go back to synthetic produce.

6. Support your rural neighbours
OK, we may be a long way from any wildlife, but we need to support our rural cousins and square up to the destruction of the countryside. Intensive farming in the UK has been nothing short of an environmental nightmare, and even we urbanites need to help to redress this in some way. Dramatic soil erosion, loss of wildlife (up 70% of wild birds have been lost in some areas), the destruction of ancient hedgerows and near extinction of some butterflies, frogs, grass-snakes and wild mammals, is the price we have all paid for the modern agricultural system.

7. Increase availability and competitive pricing of organic food
Organic sceptics seize on the cost of organic food as evidence that we are being duped into paying twice as much for food when we can't scientifically prove it's better for us. The counter-argument highlights the false economy of buying into conventional farming. It is not that organic

food is too dear, but that conventional food is too cheap. We also pay in other ways—we have to spend millions on cleaning up the agrochemicals that find their way into the water supply. It is estimated that the BSE crisis cost around £4 billion, which doesn't seem to be much of a bargain either. And eventually, an increased demand for organic produce should lead to more suppliers and bring the cost down.

8. Help protect farm workers

Not surprisingly, farm workers subjected to agrochemicals suffer significantly higher incidences of serious health problems (including cancer and respiratory problems) than those working on organic farms. This is particularly prevalent in developing countries, which gives us some perspective on the true cost of knocking a few pence off the weekly shopping bill.

9. Make up for lost time

If you're over 35, the chances are that you were raised on the remnants of a good old-fashioned diet before intensive farming practices kicked in. This is positive news, as you have a good, healthy foundation to build on. For those of us who are younger, we have been raised during a time of intensive farming, which necessitates an even greater awareness about what we consume now. Unless your parents were organic practitioners back then (and a few might have been), eating up your greens may not have been as beneficial as previously thought.

10. Safeguard the future

Part of a green outlook involves safeguarding the environment for the future. Organic farming promises to do just this. Even though we live in the city, by supporting an ecologically harmonious way of growing our food we are contributing to rural sustainability. Without our support there is a very real danger that the countryside will become a wasteland unable to support either people or wildlife.

FOOD MILES

It's not just pop stars and business executives who clock up airmiles: a vast amount of the food in our supermarkets and elsewhere has been on a global tour before ending up on the shelves. Even where produce comes from the UK, a centralized farming industry means that it could well have racked up a substantial amount of road miles before turning up in a town near you. Whilst 'save the planet, eat organic' has a certain ring to it, if the organic food has been flown half way round the world that negates many of the positive aspects. Therefore we also need to add the prefix of 'local' to our wish list. Buying from local producers and eating fresh, seasonal produce ensures that we know exactly where the produce comes from and enables us to reduce transport pollution. Of course, if you fancy a kiwi fruit you won't be able to get one from a UK farmer, but it's all about making informed decisions.

WHERE TO FIND ALL THIS LOCAL, CERTIFIED ORGANIC PRODUCE

Cutting the cord to the convenience food in the freezer, supermarket or local shop is a daunting prospect, so it's important to have lots of alternatives lined up. Finding some new solutions can even be liberating! Being a slave to one store can sometimes be a false convenience, not to mention false economy. However, increasingly you will notice that organic options are springing up in these very stores. Never keen to miss out on their slice of the pie, supermarkets are responding to consumers' desires and handing over shelf space to organic alternatives. Nor have they been slow to pick up on the need for local produce, as their nationwide policy gives way to specialist lines offering regional produce (in November 2000, Sainsburys picked up the Soil Association Award for Organic Supermarket of the Year). However, we also know that supermarkets don't deal in altruism, and independent surveys have revealed that organic produce in mainstream supermarkets can work out up to 50% more expensive than buying from other sources. Many organic suppliers are also sceptical of the motives of big retail organizations, which they feel have at least perpetuated, and in some cases created, intensive agricultural practices with their demands for bulk supply at low cost. So it seems that while supermarket organic ranges might be a convenient solution, there are plenty of other, more diverse options for canny green consumers—which is, after all, what we are aiming to become!

BOXING CLEVER

Box schemes offer the perfect solution to obtaining fresh, local produce with the minimum of inconvenience. After all, what could be more handy than having your weekly organic shopping delivered to your home, office or an agreed drop-off point? The first official box scheme started about ten years ago, but nowadays there are over 400 schemes providing food

The girls from Capricorn Organics on a delivery round in South London. Their box scheme aims to provide a more varied selection of fresh organic produce than the local supermarket.

for around 50,000 people all over the country, especially in urban areas. From humble beginnings, the box scheme has developed into an efficient, clever way of selling straight from farmer to consumer. Schemes vary in their details, but the essential idea is to order a box (which can also take the form of a bag or net) which varies in size: you can usually choose from small, medium and large boxes of fresh, organic vegetables, ranging from about £5–£15. Some box schemes offer a seasonal mix; this increases the element of surprise, and relies on willingness on your part to experiment with new recipes, as you never know exactly what you will be getting. Others allow you to pick exactly what you require—just like providing a shopping list, so that you can be sure of what you are getting. At the moment UK producers only provide 30% of the organic food we consume, so during the spring months while crops are growing, some suppliers may have to source organic produce that is less local.

Be prepared to try a few different box schemes until you find one that works well for you. Get your hands on *The Organic Directory,* so that you can find one that delivers to your area. Some users complain that standards fluctuate; the Soil Association has launched a new award scheme for the best box schemes, which will help you to choose a good one. You should also make sure that you are getting good quality produce. Allowing for the fact that organic produce won't be uniformly round, pert and perfectly formed, it should still be good quality. In larger cities, where there is competition for good produce, make sure the supplier isn't sending all the best stuff to a retail outlet or restaurant.

ORGANIC SPECIALISTS

Trends always have their followers, and the organic scene is no exception. Not surprisingly, due to the impact of the organic movement, a number of specialist, dedicated stores have sprouted up around the UK. This is especially good news for urbanites, as these stores are almost exclusively in towns and cities (we are expecting to get another one on our doorstep any day now). Stores such as Fresh & Wild, which is planning to increase its number of stores and to venture outside London, and other long-standing stores like Planet Organic, provide a haven for the discerning, informed customer who wants to buy organic produce and green products. These are also good places to start the transition to organic food. The staff there are very knowledgeable and should be able to answer any questions, and there is plenty of literature to tell you what's going on. You'll also be able to find a host of certified products so that you can start to recognize the labels that you need to

Fresh veg at Fresh & Wild.

watch out for. Smaller health food shops have also raised their game, taking advantage of an increased variety of organic and green products to match the growth of interest among consumers. You'll find everything from toiletries and cosmetics to books, confectionery, dairy products and pastas. It's certainly enough to rival a conventional shopping experience.

NET WORKING

If you haven't got a mecca of organic shopping to rival Fresh & Wild or Planet Organic in your town centre yet, you can always explore internet options. Not only should you find box schemes (see the online Organic Directory at <www.theorganicdirectory.co.uk>, and try other search engines for local schemes), but there are also a number of opportunities to buy direct from the producers. <www.realproduce.co.uk> features producers from all over the country, cutting out the middleman to offer you a direct route to cheeses, chocolates, seafood or seasonal produce. Though not necessarily organic, the produce is directly from the producer.

FARMERS' MARKETS

Farmers' Markets seem to be the latest accessory for any discerning town. They are springing up all over the place, from the suburbs to the inner cities. Ten new markets have emerged in London alone in the last year, and it's no longer a novelty to see a sign advertising a weekend market in a nearby urban space. Whilst some of these ventures are reinstating old traditional markets that would have existed some years back, many are new ventures, allowing farmers to get their produce into areas for the first time. The contemporary emphasis on fresh, local produce, some of which is organic, gives us yet another option for weekly shopping, or at least a place where we can supplement the core items with a few interesting extras.

The idea behind a farmers' market is that growers and producers from the local area—in the case of a large city, this can be quite a few miles away—come in person to sell their own produce straight to the customer. Whatever the stallholder is selling should have been grown, made, produced or reared by them. This is a perfect set-up for city customers: not only has does this fresh, local produce arrive on our doorstep, but it comes with someone who can answer any queries we may have.

As the produce is local it will obviously change with the seasons, but this is all part of the experience and the challenge (remember you can always reach for that recipe book). Much of the produce is organic—if you are not sure, ask the stallholder for certification. Around 120 farmers' markets have popped up all over the UK in the last year, proving that a large amount of the British public like what they find there and are keen to support small farming operations.

Visit <www.farmersmarkets.co.uk> to get information on your local farmers' market, or phone 01225 787 914. Londoners can call 020 7704 9659 or visit <www.londonfarmers.com> for information on markets in the capital.

LABEL QUEEN

If you are a label junkie who has dedicated many hours to scouring clothes shops, flea markets and junk shops for that all important find, then your skills will stand you in good stead for buying organic produce.

Food shopping may require you to be a little more alert than previously. Take a look at dedicated organic foodstores to begin with. These range from your local health food shop, which you may have walked past hundreds of times, to the specialist shops already mentioned, like Fresh & Wild and Planet Organic. Their knowledgeable staff are on hand to help you sort the wheat from the chaff (quite literally).

WHAT'S IN A NAME?

In this case, not very much. A quasi-green name dreamed up by marketing departments conjuring up images of happy little rabbits, forests and flowers, doesn't mean that the product is any more healthy, environmentally conscious or beneficial than the products you are trying to avoid. Beware of fake labels too—symbols depicting caterpillars, butterflies, birds etc don't count for anything if they're not the official labels (see guide below).

Remember that the whole point of shopping for organic produce is so that you can be confident of the route from farmer to table. That's why it's important to buy certified produce. Certification bodies exist to keep organic standards high and to ensure that we consumers are not getting ripped off. Registered products need to be grown and produced in accordance with strict organic conditions. If you are buying loose produce like fruit and veg, then the supplier should be in possession of certification to prove that the produce is indeed organic.

A QUICK GUIDE TO LABELS

A quick look at the shelves or packets should reveal one or more of the following symbols. If there is no symbol, you should see the equivalent European Certifying Authority listed.

Soil Association: UK5
This is the symbol you will see on most organic produce as the Soil Association now certifies around 70% of organic food produced in the UK. As the SA sets such stringent standards, you can be confident that anything you buy sporting its symbol will be top quality organic produce.

UKROFS: UK1

This collection of letters means the United Kingdom Register of Organic Food Standards: all manufacturers or suppliers who want to be known as organic must conform to the UKROFS standards, which follow the guidelines set up by the European Community in 1993.

The Organic Food Federation: UK4

Products carrying this symbol conform to UKROFS standards. This organization represents an independent group of producers who are keen to display to the public that their products are organic.

Organic Farmers and Growers Ltd: UK2

Again these standards conform to UKROFS. This is essentially a co-operative of farmers and growers, most of whom also belong to the Soil Association.

Demeter: UK6

This is the symbol of the Bio-Dynamic Agricultural Association. This is organic with a capital 'O', and is also known as 'organic plus'. As biodynamic farming requires people, earth and universe to function in harmony and takes account of cosmic forces, organic principles are absolutely central to the philosophy.

Scottish Organic Producers Association: UK3

A co-operative for farmers and growers in the Scottish regions, following UKROFS guidelines.

The Irish Organic Farmers and Growers: UK7

As well as the standards laid down by UKROFS, this organization has some additional stipulations.

Other labels you might see include:

The Organic Food Awards—this means that the product or scheme has won or been highly commended in awards designed to recognize outstanding schemes.

The Fair Trade Logo—this is not necessarily an organic product, but one that has been made in accordance with fair trade regulations. This means that the small farmer, producer or plantation worker has secured a fair price for the product. It stops us taking advantage of workers in developing countries.

GM-Free: This indicates that the food is free from genetically modified ingredients. As we cannot be sure that important food staples such as soya are not GM-free, this label is sadly a very good idea.

Remember that if your health shop or organic store sells organic produce from abroad, the signs and symbols may differ as standards tend to vary from country to country. Ask the retailer for some advice.

CONVENIENCE KINGS

Fortunately for the culinary challenged amongst us, it is still possible to implement a more organic diet without making everything from scratch out of your seasonal box of fruit and veg. A proliferation of brands and products means that you can easily find a wide range of organic ready-made convenience foods that require absolutely no catering skills and very little time. Companies such as Whole Earth Foods produce a whole range of cereals, chilled and frozen meals and ready-made sauces which can help smooth the transition to an organic-based diet. Unlike conventional convenience products, these ranges are

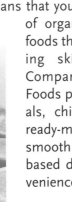

ORGANIC
fennel
seed
origin
EGYPT
£ 1.59 / 100g

4824 ORGANIC CERTIFICATION

not full of emulsifiers and preservatives, and the overall ingredients are of a high standard. However, they obviously work out more costly and are best integrated into an overall diet which includes plenty of fresh fruit and veg. A vast range of organic chocolates (Green & Blacks have an especially good reputation), biscuits and cakes ensures that we don't have to give up all our vices. However, it's important to remember that just because it's organic, it doesn't mean that it's infused with goodness. Sugar and fat still need to be eaten in moderation, so you will have to check the labels, especially if you're on any kind of weight loss programme.

TOP TIPS ON FOOD

As most 'fresh' produce in supermarkets is covered in various preservatives, you might be slightly unnerved by how quickly natural foods go past their best. Since nobody enjoys spending their leisure time cleaning rotten food out of the bottom of the fridge or fruit bowl, a few kitchen tips might help you to prolong your weekly shop or box delivery:

• Check the temperature in your fridge. The coldest part should be between 0–5°C. Too cold and you could partially freeze the food, too hot and it won't be properly chilled.

• Also watch the temperature in the freezer, which should be around –18°C. You will probably want to invest in a thermometer to check this.

• Invest in a good freezer, and freeze fresh produce on the day you buy it (if you aren't able to eat it all fresh). Blanch vegetables before freezing to preserve the bulk of the nutrients and keep them fresh (place them in a colander and lower them into boiling water until the colour sharpens, then dunk them into cold water). If you grow your own produce (see Chapter 3) you should freeze the excess on the day you pick it.

• Make herb cubes. Place fresh, chopped herbs into an ice cube tray with a squirt of water and leave to freeze. When you come to cook you can just add a cube for instant fresh herbs.

Be mega-organized. A good old-fashioned list is the way forward to a healthy, cost-effective organic diet. If you don't plan meals, you will buy too much, forget stuff or just buy too little. You will also be able to effectively manage your cupboards and fridge, knowing what is fresh and when it should be eaten. Don't worry—it shouldn't infringe on your time too much. It might take a little practice, but keeping lists and planning ahead will liberate you from having to come up with last minute options, and it will make your diet—and the amount you spend on it—easier to control.

diary

Mealtimes in our flat tend to be rather sporadic arrangements which revolve around how busy we are, who's had a chance to do the shopping, and what we feel like eating. Our traditional shopping arrangements are uninspired, expensive and do not give us the opportunity to maintain the well balanced, healthy diet that we are all looking for. We invariably end up running into the supermarket next to the station on the way back from work just before it closes, and grabbing at some form of convenience food or even, horror or horrors, resorting to one of the many take-aways which have sprung up around us. Unfortunately none of these practices is conducive to a healthy or interesting diet, and the lack of planning means that it can also work out to be quite expensive. But in the interests of research we embrace the opportunity to abandon our entrenched habits and spend two weeks finding something less boring (and organic) instead. . . .

As an introduction to green shopping and eating, we decided to break ourselves in gently. To cut the umbilical cord to our usual haunts with the minimum of fuss, we take a trip to a recently opened branch of a specialist organic retailer which is fairly close to us. Initially this a good way to start, as, like a conventional supermarket, everything is under the same roof. Large organic and green specialist stores are becoming increasingly common, but there are also a number of good quality independent stores all over the UK which stock a wide array of organic products.

We were immediately impressed by the lively atmosphere, and being slightly hung over from the previous night the juice bar was particularly enticing. They juice the fruit and vegetables in front of you, which is quite satisfying to watch, although time-consuming if you happened to be in a rush. Better still, for people like us in search of something tasty with the minimum of personal effort, there are delicious food counters filled with things like tortillas, vegetarian kebabs and stuffed peppers. Needless to say, we ended up buying a few of these delights to take home with us before we had even ventured to the grocery aisles.

Once we tore ourselves away from the juice bar and deli, we were immediately struck by the sheer range of products on the shelves. There seemed to

diary

be at least two or three alternatives to everything you would find in your common-or-garden supermarket. We were quickly forced to abandon the

basket we had picked up and get a fully fledged trolley. Product displays, such as a promotion for an organic picnic, proved to be particularly alluring, and we tended to buy more of these items than the core products we should have been purchasing. We emerged after spending a good two hours, just under £60, and with a large amount of carrier bags (these are redeemable off your next shopping trip—5p

per bag), but without some of the core items we should have bought to start stocking the cupboards.

Unfortunately, by Wednesday the cupboards and fridge were looking bare again. One of the problems of buying ready-made food, particularly very tasty ready-made food, is that it tends to get eaten immediately. I had to agree with Ben that a more systematic approach, and perhaps a list, might be necessary next time. By now it had also become apparent that we were slipping back into our old ways. A culmination of a busy period at work and an abundance of social engagements was taking its toll on our good intentions, and those convenience food cartons were starting to mount up again. We had reverted to our usual haunt of the supermarket, but at least this time we were also trying out their organic lines. Although these have increased, they're still quite expensive, and there is nowhere near as much variety as in a specialist retailer. Determined to pull us back from the brink of failure, I turned to The Organic Directory for help and found some box schemes that deliver to our area in South London. This is particularly easy for us: Ben works from home, so they can deliver at any time during the day. We decided to start as soon as possible, so on Thursday morning I phoned through an order for a basic box of vegetables.

It was here that our great scheme came unstuck—the box wasn't delivered until 7.30pm on Friday, leaving us box scheme novices (and cooks of limited ability) with no time to plan a meal. To add insult to injury, the contents of the box did not seem to be in the first flush of youth. Whilst Ben wondered

diary

whether this was just symptomatic of organic food, and had only taken us by surprise because we were used to unnaturally perfect food that never goes off, I am inclined to think we have been sent the dregs.

Although we could easily have raised the problems with the contents and time of our delivery with the operators, we elected, in the interests of yet more research, to try another scheme. This time we opted for a small, local concern (it has also recently developed an online shopping list, which will be very convenient for the future). However, I chose to place the first order by phone. This was worthwhile, especially for a first order, because the girls that ran the scheme were very knowledgeable and helpful, and able to tell you what they would be trying to put in a mixed box of fruit and veg. In addition, you can also order groceries and household items, which is pretty convenient.

On Wednesday the latest box arrived. The fruit and vegetables were superior quality, very fresh and there was a good mix. As an added incentive we were also given a free small bag of potatoes. We immediately started thinking about our next order, and how we might well branch out to a few more groceries which can be ordered in. Another excellent feature of this small service is that the suppliers get to know your orders and go themselves to select produce from the organic warehouses. As this scheme tries to use only local organic produce (and British produce where possible), when certain items aren't available they'll be able to make a good guess at what you would like in its place. My sister has taken pity on my lack of culinary prowess and lent me a basic vegetarian cookbook which, although I'm not a vegetarian, will give me some ideas about how to use up the contents of the veg box.

On Saturday afternoon I ventured down to Borough Market—one of the oldest markets in London, now under threat from proposed railway developments. The sheer quantity of different growers and the plethora of foodstuffs here is quite awesome. Although this is not a specifically organic market, there seems to be lots of clearly marked organic produce. There is a good bustling atmosphere here, and the majority of stallholders are only too happy to tell you about their products. In fact, as there are a number of TV crews jostling for space and TV chefs wandering about, you would suppose that stallholders are pretty used to speaking eloquently about their products. The market is apparently known as 'the Larder of London', and small wonder, as everything seems to be available—from hundreds of different cheeses, apples and pears to specialist apple juices and ciders, to sumptuous cakes and oak-smoked garlic. My final purchases were designed to liven up the contents of our box at home: they included the oak-smoked garlic, a variety of herbs and some blue cheese. Then it was off home to pore over my new recipe book!

funky farmer

A new breed of farmer is capitalizing on old methods and a new enthusiasm for fresh, local food. . . .

Not even the most hardcore urbanite can be oblivious to the crises that have devastated some British farming communities. However, it's not all doom and gloom. Thirty-one year old Sam Webb is one farmer who doesn't fit the traditional mould, and her farm in Kent is a good example of how a contemporary outlook can embrace the organic movement and even save a family farming tradition.

The Webb's business is cobnuts—a little known but indigenous tasty English nut which thanks to our new desire for all things natural and homegrown is experiencing a resurgence in popularity. Sam frequently drives the short trip up to London with a crop of nuts for some of the farmers' markets. The unusual family cobnut tradition was begun by Sam's great-aunt when, as a tenant, she bought the farm over one hundred years ago. The farm boasts three thousand cobnut trees, making them the largest single producer. No chemical sprays have been used on the crop over the many years they have been cultivating cobnuts, during which time the farm has passed from Sam's great-aunt to her mother, Gill Webb.

Sam and her boyfriend Chris moved back to Kent from London to live on the farm and to pitch in and keep it going with Gill. Both Sam and Chris felt that they had done their time in London, and despite the fact that Chris had never lived in a rural area, let alone on a farm, they decided to give it a go. However they have not abandoned their city habits entirely, which is lucky given that farming is not as profitable as it once was. Ironically, for a farm where electricity is a relatively recent phenomenon and where only very basic modernization has occurred, it's become something of a hub of technological activity. Chris, a musician, takes a break from trimming sheep hooves to work on his latest track, while Sam juggles her alternative career as an interactive designer and sometime yoga teacher.

They have now achieved organic accreditation, as well as a Countryside Stewardship to help preserve the precious cobnut trees. Suppliers have been eager to snap up their organic cherries, and London restaurants are happily buying up their organically reared lambs. Altogether, things are looking good for the farm and perhaps they can look forward to the days when they really can give up the day jobs!

Information on cobnuts is available from: <www.cobnuts.co.uk> or Tel: 01732 810 263.

Chapter 3

growing
without pains

TIME FOR THE GOOD LIFE

There is of course a sure fire way to ensure that the produce on your table is fresh, local and truly organic—grow your own! If this instantly conjures up images of turning over your precious garden to all manner of vegetables, pigs and goats in a manic recreation of The Good Life, fear not! It's a much better idea to implement small, sustainable changes, rather than jump in with extravagant gestures only to regret it later. If you don't have any outside space that you can commandeer for your new gardening project, you can always grow some herbs in containers or in a window box. Even this simple gesture will give you fresh, interesting herbs that will jazz up the contents of a box scheme delivery and help to extend your organic food repertoire even further. However limited your space, you are bound to find a spot somewhere where you can raise a crop of healthy herbs, a few tomatoes or a pepper plant, so you can experience first-hand the taste revolution of home grown produce.

SPACE HOPPING

It's time to start spotting potential in the most unlikely corner of your yard, patio or balcony—or even that of one of your friend's—in an effort to seek out some opportunities for planting and growing. If you haven't taken much interest in outdoor pursuits up until now, this might seem strange at first, but assessing the potential in a bit of stray garden can become strangely compulsive!

Horticultural losers and gardening dunces take note: it's not rocket science! A bit of knowledge, perseverance and a few containers could see you reaping some organically grown, fresh produce from your own balcony.

Growing your own needn't mean a recreation of The Good Life. Any outside space will do, such as a few containers on a balcony or a window box.

It won't come as a big shock to learn that we have lost more and more of our urban green space to housing, car parks, supermarkets and other space-devouring concerns. Using London as a pertinent example, at one time most of the capital was fed from produce brought in from the west of the city, but then that space became Heathrow. This area still supplies the bulk of our food, but only after it has been flown thousands of miles across the world. Until recently, 'progress' meant sacrificing our precious urban space—and losing a fragile ecosystem and any semblance of biodiversity. This malaise finally filters down to us urbanites, until ultimately we lose both the opportunity and the will to plant and grow, and wave goodbye to our chance to create a greener urban environment.

In recent years, many groups of urbanites have begun to stand up for their green spaces and their opportunities to grow and plant. Community gardens, green space projects and city farms are all fighting to preserve our precious green spaces. For the uninitiated gardener, these kinds of schemes can provide a lifeline, giving the less than green-fingered an opportunity to pick up some new skills and experience the satisfaction of growing and planting in an outdoor space.

As you will have noticed, we're now a nation of gardening obsessives. You can't turn on the TV without seeing a gardening programme, and there has been a proliferation of magazines and books to accompany and feed our new-found interest. However, this hasn't signalled a boom in vegetable plots, with us all becoming self-sufficient. New garden fashions tend to view any outside space as an extension of the interior, to be covered in decking and gravel—in some gardens there is very little evidence of nature at all. However, even dedicated followers of garden fashion can get involved with growing, and bring some of the green life back with some container gardening—pots of herbs will brighten up the decking!

GUERRILLA GARDENING

If you fancy a more militant approach to reclaiming your space and your right to grow in the urban outdoors, then you should take inspiration from proponents of Guerrilla Gardening. This is one group of urbanites who are determined to shake up our apathy and plant where ever they find an opportunity.

Graham Burnett, a leading light in Guerrilla Gardening, assesses the space all around him to find a spot ripe for a bit of 'clandestine cultivation'. At the heart of this movement is the belief that in order to have control over our own lives, we must have the ability to produce our own food. The Guerrillas exercise what they see as their natural rights to grow herbs and vegetables everywhere—from city roundabouts to railway embankments—in order to defy capitalism and break free of the cycle of supply and demand.

Even if you don't subscribe to all their beliefs, you can take a leaf out of the GG's book and "apply a little vision to the land around you". Whether you are growing a tub of herbs on a balcony or converting an old rose bed to a useful vegetable patch, you can enjoy the freedom of growing your own food.

URBAN LAND ARMY

If the only thing holding you back from becoming a supreme green gardener is the fact that you are seriously stuck for space, there is another solution. An allotment could well be the answer you are looking for. Initially a scheme to help the war effort, allotment culture has been brought to our attention by the deeply unglamorous Arthur Fowler on Eastenders. But don't be deterred by the allotment's frumpy image— these days all kinds of people of all different ages are taking advantage of very low cost space near to their urban homes, where a bit of hard graft and trial and error can see them bringing in their own produce. Unbelievably, most allotments are undersubscribed, and some are even in danger of closing. Contact your local council, ask to speak to the allotments officer, and snap one up before they become this year's must have and you have to join a waiting list.

ALLOTMENT FRENZY

Todd Weller explains why he's been putting in so many hours on a Walthamstow allotment.

I started thinking about growing things again about two years ago. I think it was after going on holiday somewhere—when I came back to England and kept buying premium tomatoes from the supermarket that just didn't taste of anything. I grew up on a farm in Wiltshire and there was always a domestic crop so I have that memory too—of things like a proper potato.

I caught sight of the allotments when I went to a car boot sale and spotted them near the Town Hall. They were just close enough to my house, which is really important, because if it's a real trek to get there and you have to drive miles, it really negates the point of having one in the first place. It was quite straightforward once I'd decided I really wanted to grow some vegetables. I phoned the allotment officer at my local borough—some allotments are controlled directly by the borough and some have been contracted out. I assumed I would have to join a waiting list, but to my surprise I found out that only 20% of the allotments in our area are taken.

It takes a lot of hard work and knowledge to run a successful allotment and I've still got a lot to learn! This year I had to decide whether to go for it or give it up. So I've completely cleared the weeds and I'm going to get a Rotavator to speed the whole process up a bit. I've also built a shed so that I don't have to bring everything with me all the time.

Quantity is the biggest problem at the moment. I need to extend the growing time rather than having a huge quantity at the same time. You forget the power of the soil—if you don't pick a courgette on the right night, it's a marrow! You also have to be careful what you put in the compost. It's probably easier to make compost in your own home than on the allotment. An allotment is also a brilliant way of picking up tips from growers who have had plots there for years.

It is just amazing to be able to finish work, go down to the allotment on the scooter, lift the vegetables and cook them within 20 minutes knowing they're all organic.

It especially suits me because I've always shopped daily: I think you should think about what you feel you should eat. The first year I thought "I can't do this, it's too much." But the first crop of strawberries makes you realize why you are doing it.

Four green gardening no-nos to be avoided at all costs:

• **Wasting water:** the cardinal sin of anti-green gardening involves using hosepipes or sprinkler system.
Solution: Most of the time we get plenty of rain in the UK so invest in, or make, a water butt to collect water from your guttering. Alternatively, use your bath water (minus the bubble bath) to water plants and lawns.

• **Using peat compost**: Hands off our natural peat bogs, which are being depleted at an alarming rate taking a fragile ecosystem with them.
Solution: Read on for tips on starting your own organic compost bin or on where to buy organic compost that is 100% renewable.

• **Buying lots of new plastic seed trays**. There are lots of pots and containers around that will make great new homes for plants, so get recycling and try not to use new plastic items.

• **Using chemical fertilizers and pest repellents:** Obviously green gardening can't condone the use of chemicals. Remember even so-called new eco-friendly slug pellets can kill other wildlife like hedgehogs.
Solution: There are plenty of natural alternatives like calcified seaweed to enrich your soil but keep your growing space pure. Read on for some tips on getting rid of slugs.

GROWING IN THE WORLD'S SMALLEST GARDEN

Once you've decided it's a nice idea, it's time to move on to the practicalities and actually rise to the challenge of growing something. This is our step-by-step diary guide to growing a few basics with no prior knowledge and the minimum of fuss.

The idea:
In the spirit of research, we were very keen to try and grow some of our own fresh, organic produce. However, given the rather restricted nature of our flat this was a fairly daunting task.

1) First step: Assess the space
Ben and I trundle out to assess our outdoor space. We actually part-own a small garden which is part of a large divided garden at the back of the house, as well as a balcony which gets a lot of sun. There is no direct access to the garden from the house, as you need to leave the house by the front door downstairs and then walk round the back. Although not fantastically convenient, it provides a good space to get

everything sorted out and of course to get soil from. However, as there is no ground space for a small vegetable garden, we decide to stick to container gardening—using a collection of pots and hanging baskets. We figure that these can then go on the balcony, where we can easily water them, they'll be sheltered from the wind and will get lots of sunlight.

2) Deciding what to grow

Our neighbours and co-garden-owners are surprisingly enthusiastic about our little gardening project, and we all decide we're looking forward to harvesting our own abundant crops in a few weeks' time. Ben suggests that we need to grow herbs and vegetables that we can add to the contents of our box scheme deliveries. We decide what our crops are going to be: a selection of herbs, cherry tomatoes, sprouting broccoli, lamb's lettuce, rocket and chillies.

3) Getting started

I look around for some pots in the garden centre and find a bargain in the form of four pebble pots for £9.99 (second-hand), ranging from 12–30 inches in diameter, and two wicker hanging baskets with a plastic lining which I pierced at the bottom to allow drainage.

4) Buying our seeds

We choose our seeds from an accredited organic catalogue where the organic seeds are clearly marked. This way we are 100% certain that we are growing totally organic produce. We choose:

•   Tumbler tomatoes— these are apparently excellent for hanging baskets and containers, are ready early in the summer, and each plant produces around 4 lbs of sweet cherry tomatoes.

•   Heatwave chillies (very hot) and ornamental red, yellow and orange chillies so that they will also have some aesthetic appeal.

•   Herbs—Flat and curl left parsley, chives, oregano, golden oregano (marjoram), basil, coriander, mint, bay leaf, fennel, chervil and sage.

Forward to early spring . . .

4) Compost and seed trays
Our seeds arrive from the catalogue, and we pick up some multi-purpose organic compost from the garden centre which is 100% peat-free. We sow small quantities of seeds—we only have limited space, so we won't need lots of plants. In fact we only use half of each packet.

In the absence of any seed trays, we make use of a series of plant pots and recycled boxes (we recycled plastic egg boxes, and just made a small hole in the bottom of each for drainage).

5) Sowing the seeds
Next, I fill the trays with organic compost, and get some tips from a book on gardening for idiots which tells me to gently firm it down with my fingers at first and then use the bottom of the plant pot (or any other flat object) to flatten it down again. This levels out the compost about $1/4$" from the top of the container.

Next the fun bit—scattering the seed over the surface. Then I cover with a thin layer of compost and gently water and cover with a clear plastic bag (recycled, of course!)

6) Leaving the seeds to germinate
We put the containers on the window sill in the kitchen which is perfect as the sunlight through there is not too strong. The recommended temperature is 13°–18°C (55°–66°F). After this, it's just a question of keeping the trays moist, but not to the point of saturating them. I have come up with the ingenious idea (well, I think so anyway) of recycling a kitchen spray bottle (well washed out) to spray the trays.

We leave the seeds for just over two weeks until there are signs of germination.

Forward two weeks . . .

7) Give the seedlings light
I can see emerging shoots, so I take the covers off. This allows the seedlings as much light as possible.

Forward one week . . .

8) Spacing out the seedlings
Another week has passed and the seedlings are large enough to handle, so I space them out singly in other containers which will allow them to develop into good-sized plants. We are spacing the herbs out in clumps (this will presumably make them easier to handle, especially herbs like chives).

9) Planting the herbs

The herbs have now grown to 4 or 5 inches, so I plant them into the two hanging baskets—you can use whatever kind of container you want, and remember you can put several varieties together.

10) Transplanting the rocket and lamb's lettuce

The rocket and lamb's lettuce have been kept in the seed trays and have now reached a couple of inches in height. It's time to transplant them into their final home, so I plant them three inches apart in a large pot.

11) Moving the tomatoes and chillies

My trusty reference book suggests that the tomatoes and chillies should be one plant to a small pot (which we have followed), but now they have grown to about five inches tall. I transplant three or four of them into a large pot.

REAPING THE REWARDS

I am religiously committed to watering the plants in the morning and evening, and they have grown into fine specimens. I'm also being very green with water, and using bathwater or collected rainwater to keep them nice and moist, but being careful not to over-water them—particularly the tomato plants, which might wind up with blossom end rot. The tomatoes are coming through already and I'm feeding them organic food once a week that just mixes in with the rain or bathwater.

It's mid-June, and there are loads of tomatoes. I'm extremely proud of them and they taste pretty good too. The herbs are also flourishing, and not only do they save us money but they have a lively, fresh taste which really comes through in salads and in cooking.

TOP TIPS

•   Herbs can be sown throughout the year and grown in pots on window sills.

•   Pinch out the shoots of most herbs regularly to produce compact, bushy plants.

•   Keep plants moist and avoid over- or under-watering—especially with tomato plants to avoid blossom end rot.

• Only use plant food that is certified organic, if you want to have truly organic plants.

• Don't waste water in the garden. Remember to collect rainwater or use the water from your bath. Water the plants in the early morning or in the evening, rather than in the heat of the midday sun when all the water will evaporate.

• Steer clear of slug pellets, as they go against the idea of being organic and kill other animals. Slugs are a nuisance, however, so you may have to resort to some age-old methods. Experts swear by disrupting their routines, and advise disgruntled growers to plod out into the garden at night, armed with a torch, and physically pick them off the plants. This might be messy and rather hard work, but they are apparently creatures of habit, and it may well disturb the slug community sufficiently to keep them off your plants. Alternatively, try placing a shallow saucer of beer with the rim at the same level of the soil, and the slugs will be drawn in by the beer and drown.

• Buy peat-free organic compost from garden centres, as this will help to preserve peat bogs. If you are organized enough and fancy a new gardening challenge, try making your own compost bin (see below).

THE LO-DOWN ON COMPOST

This is a brief guide to the fascinating world of compost. To the uninitiated, few things can sound less glamorous or intriguing than compost, but keen gardeners and recycling enthusiasts can waffle on about the subject for hours. Beware—your compost bin is about to become an important part of your life!

When people refer to our 'throwaway society', they aren't exaggerating. It is estimated that we manage to generate around 25 million tones of household rubbish each year. But around 30% of that is compostable, such as tea bags, vegetable peelings and food scraps.

In common with other countries around the world, we have been heavily relying on landfill sites to hide away all the rubbish we generate. These are literally massive pits where all our waste is dumped. Not surprisingly, we are now running out of space for vast landfill sites, and the land available for our rubbish decreases every year. Not only that, but once the rubbish is in the landfill, it's useless—any organic matter decomposes to produce methane (which is thought to be a strong contributor to greenhouse gas, and the resulting climate change) and leachate—a polluting liquid which can have bad effects on groundwater.

Other large-scale waste disposal schemes have tried to burn waste, but this produces carcinogens such as dioxins, which some experts suggest are responsible for up to 10% of cancers.

So with 85% of rubbish being trucked off to landfill sites, it seems our duty to compost as much as we can in our own gardens. Composting is a completely natural process, involving millions of microscopic creatures which create heat as they break down the organic matter into fine particles. The compost heap then cools down, and it's over to worms and insects to munch down through the tougher material. It's a natural way of waste disposal and soil fertilization.

Home-made compost is not just a great solution because of the environmental limitations of other forms of waste disposal, but also because it is fantastically beneficial for growing, and a good alternative to the usual peat compost—natural peat bogs take thousands of years to form, and generate their own ecosystems which need to be preserved.

BIN MAN

Compost bins can be made using all manner of discarded materials such as old tyres, timber and wire mesh. You can construct a simple frame with old pieces of wood by nailing planks to posts knocked into the ground and covering with a piece of old carpet or plastic sheeting. If you'd prefer to buy a bin rather than making your own, you'll find good deals in garden centres, on the web or even through mail order.

Compost bin from The Natural Collection

Try to have your bin in a fairly sunny area of bare soil or grass. You can also break up the earth underneath to encourage drainage. During cold spells, you might need to use what's referred to as a 'natural activator', which just means something like manure or bedding from vegetarian livestock such as rabbits, chickens or horses. This gets the compost heated up and keeps it going.

WORMERIES

If you don't have a garden and aren't squeamish, you can always build a wormery to make your own organic waste disposal unit. Worm starter kits, which are available in many shops, contain a colony of special worms such as red or tiger worms. These can be kept carefully indoors and produce small quantities of compost and a liquid plant food.

The Do's and Don'ts of Composting

Do Compost	Don't Compost
Fruit	Clothes or textiles
Vegetables	Cotton buds
Lawn mowings	Nappies
Eggshells	Large pieces of wood
Coffee grounds	Any diseased plants
Dead flowers	Dog or cat mess
Feathers	
Hair	

As for the list of things that can't be composted, check out Chapter 4 (Living La Vida Verde) for some ideas on how some of these items can be dealt with.

Members of the Community Composting Network showing that composting is, after all, a team sport.

THE URBAN JUNGLE GUIDE TO
THE ULTIMATE COMPOST

Compost fans take their art very seriously! This is an amalgamation of top tips from a number of city farmers used to small spaces, which should set you up with a fine compost bin. Otherwise you can pick up more information from the addresses at the end of this chapter or check out *Backyard Composting* by John Roulac, published by Green Books (see contacts) which will teach you everything you will ever need to know.

In your chosen bin (preferably rodent-proof), make a base of 3–4" of woody material to encourage aeration.

Alternate layers of green (nitrogen—grass, food scraps [wet], garden trimmings) and brown (carbon—fallen leaves, straw, dry newspaper strips) materials. Layers should be between 2–4". Chop up larger materials to expedite decomposition.

Whenever you add a food layer, sprinkle with soil and then finish with a brown layer to prevent smells and flies.

Mix bin contents often at least once every two weeks. This allows for air and gets the bin heating up again.

Moisture content should equal that of a wrung-out dishcloth. Only add water if the contents are very dry after mixing.

The pile will shrink. Keep adding to the bin until almost full. Place carpet or similar on surface of pile to retain heat and moisture.

Compost is ready to use when it looks like soil/peat, after approx. two to three months. However, it is good to age it for another month.

THE COMPOST COMMUNITY

Yes, compost can even help you win friends and influence people, especially in urban areas where you might not have enough organic waste or space to warrant your own compost heap or bin. If your outdoor space is formed from a large garden that has been divided up, you could always get together with the other garden owners and get a compost heap going. Alternatively The Community Composting Network (see Mini Directory) will advise you on your nearest group and provide advice and free information.

RECIPE CORNER

Here are seven easy, effective recipes to convert the fruits of your labour into brilliant meals.

So once you've grown herbs, tomatoes, salad leaves and other fantastic plants, what are you going to do with them? The following easy recipes provide some ideas to help you beef up the contents of a box scheme delivery or a trip to organic supermarket. They are quick and simple, and go with lots of variations. Remember that eggs should be certified as organic free-range, not just given a 'country'-sounding name. Wash all produce carefully before you use it.

•   Herbs used: sage, coriander, bay leaf, chives, oregano, golden oregano (marjoram), mint, parsley, fennel, chervil, basil.

•   Plants used: rocket, lamb's lettuce, purple sprouting broccoli, cherry tomatoes.

1) Ticklemore Blue Cheese Dressing [for 4–6]

Any organic, blue cheese is good in this recipe. Ticklemore is particularly tasty but you can substitute another—the more local the producer, the better. This dressing is brilliant on baked potatoes, pasta, green salads or just used as a dip. You can also serve it with the purple sprouting broccoli—just steam the broccoli.

You need:

    3 oz Ticklemore Blue cheese
    5 fl oz crème fraiche
    2 tablespoons home-made mayonnaise [or good organic brand]
    1 large clove of garlic
    1 level teaspoon salt
    1 teaspoon of wholegrain, speciality or Dijon mustard
    1 tablespoon olive oil
    1 tablespoon sunflower/walnut oil
    1 tablespoon balsamic vinegar
    1 tablespoon lemon juice
    2 tablespoons chives
    freshly ground black pepper

Crush the clove of garlic in a pestle and mortar with the teaspoon of salt and work until creamy, adding the mustard and working in. Add lemon juice and vinegar, then the oil. Mix all these ingredients carefully. Combine crème fraiche and mayonnaise in a bowl, then whisk ingredients from pestle and mortar into this. When they are mixed to perfection, crumble in the cheese and chopped chives. Season with black pepper. You can always add a little milk, single cream or water if you prefer a runnier dressing, or add less liquid if it needs to be thicker.

2) Basic Vinaigrette

You can use this classic beauty on all kinds of salads—including bean and pasta salads. Or you can toss freshly steamed summer vegetables in it and add chopped green herbs, lemon zest and a little olive oil. It's also pretty good on new baby potatoes.

> 150 ml [5 fl oz] sunflower/groundnut oil
> 1 tablespoon olive or walnut oil
> 40 ml [1½ fl oz] of white/red wine vinegar/balsamic vinegar
> ½ teaspoon muscovado or brown sugar
> ½ teaspoon sea salt
> freshly milled black pepper
> 1 teaspoon Dijon mustard
> 1 crushed clove garlic [leave whole to flavour dressing]

This couldn't be easier! Just mix all the ingredients together. The best way to do this is to get your hands on a whisk or just use an empty, clean screw top jar. Remember you can always vary this dressing and add chopped chilli for a bit of spice, or chopped fresh herbs, or even lemon or lime zest—the sky's the limit!

3) Fresh Tomato Sauce

Another versatile little number. It's most obvious use is on pasta, but it also goes great with grilled or baked fish, mussels, courgettes and aubergines.

> 1 kilo [2.2 lbs] tomatoes
> 1 red onion finely chopped
> 2 cloves garlic [1 if very large]
> 1 tablespoon olive oil
> fresh basil leaves
> ½ teaspoon brown/muscovado sugar
> sea salt and freshly ground black pepper
> 2 teaspoons sun-dried tomato paste

Heat the oil in a heavy saucepan and sauté finely chopped onion and garlic over a low heat until they are very soft but not brown (this will probably take about 10 minutes). Whilst the onion is cooking, wash and chop the tomatoes. Because the tomatoes are organic there's no need to skin them as they'll add to the flavour—even more convenience! Add the tomatoes to the pan on a medium high heat until they are all happily bubbling away. You could even add a little organic wine at this point. Turn down the heat and simmer with the lid on the pan. The idea is to reduce the tomatoes down to a thickish sauce—it takes about 30 minutes to do this. After 15 minutes (i.e. half way through) add the salt, black pepper and sun dried tomato paste. If you like a strong flavour, add a dessertspoon of organic vegetable bouillon powder. Reduce for a further 15 minutes and there you go—a delicious organic sauce. Add a handful of torn basil leaves.

If you want to really get into the Italian vibe, you can vary the sauce and try:

Amatricana: Just sauté a chopped de-seeded chilli (or chillies if you like fiery food) and chopped pancetta (obviously not an option for our vegetarian friends) with the onion and garlic.

Or **Puttanesca** (translated as whore's spaghetti—make up your own jokes). Do all the chilli bit (as above), then add 100 ml (4 fl oz) of chopped pitted black olives and a small jar or tin of anchovies, 1 heaped tablespoon of capers (vegetarians can use another tablespoon of capers instead of the anchovies).

4) Salsa di peperoncino e limone (that's chilli and lemon sauce)
A handy sauce which is great with grilled fish, chicken, seafood and scallops. Or you can toss vegetables in it before roasting, or use it as a dressing on freshly steamed vegetables.

    3–4 green or red mild chillies
    4 fl oz extra virgin olive oil
    1 unwaxed lemon
    sea salt and freshly ground black pepper

De-seed and finely chop the chillies. Mix with olive oil, salt and pepper and grated lemon zest [no pith please—it's not good here]. If you can restrain yourself from pouring it on everything, it is really good when it's been left for several hours and the flavours have developed.

5) Salsa Verde
Delicious with a host of different vegetables, salads, fish, chicken, goat's cheese, pasta and polenta. Don't worry too much about which green herbs you use here—you can make use of whatever you have.

Large bunch of flat leaf parsley without stalks
Bunch of fresh basil leaves without stalks
A few fresh mint leaves
3 garlic cloves
50 g [2 oz] salted capers [optional]
4 anchovy fillets [optional]
1 tablespoon Dijon mustard
2 tablespoons red wine vinegar
6 tablespoons extra virgin olive oil
Sea salt and freshly ground black pepper

A little green test coming up here: do you a) finely chop all the herbs, garlic, capers and anchovies by hand on a chopping board, or b) whizz them through the processor. When you've made your decision, empty into a large bowl and add the vinegar. Pour in the olive oil gradually whilst continually stirring. Mix in the mustard and adjust the seasoning to your own taste. If you omit the capers and anchovies you will need to add more salt to compensate. Finally, don't forget the pepper.

6) Basic Mayonnaise

Now this really is 'miracle mayo', because it's so easy and you know exactly what's gone into it. There are of course zillions of uses for mayonnaise: from fish, vegetables and chicken, to chips (organic potatoes and sunflower oil) and potato wedges. Remember that even organic mayonnaise is highly calorific and should be used sparingly!

These ingredients will make 300ml [1/2 pint]:

2 organic free-range egg yolks
1/2 teaspoon salt
1 teaspoon Dijon mustard
Freshly ground black pepper
2 teaspoons white wine vinegar
300ml [1/2 pint] extra virgin olive oil

Keep all the ingredients at room temperature so that the mayonnaise doesn't curdle. Put the egg yolks, vinegar and salt into a mixing bowl and place it on top of a damp tea towel to prevent the bowl from slipping whilst whisking. Using a wire whisk, gradually beat the olive oil into the egg mixture a little at a time until it is all incorporated. When you have very carefully added about half of the oil you can add the rest whilst you speed up the whisking (but keep it going continually!).

Here's another recipe that's easy to vary:

Aioli

Just mix 3–4 garlic cloves with basic mayonnaise for a distinctly Spanish flavour. Crush garlic with the flat side of a knife blade, using the widest part—keep the skin on the garlic, as it's less likely to slip. Remove the skin, sprinkle with a little salt, mash and mix with the mayo.

Basil Mayonnaise

Add garlic as above, and a good handful of finely torn basil leaves.

7) Tomato and Coriander Salsa

This is a natural with char-grilled tuna—you can add some mayonnaise as well. Alternatively it's brilliant mixed with beans and with Mexican inspired food.

450 g [1 lb] of firm tomatoes
1 small red onion finely chopped
1 green chilli de-seeded and chopped
bunch of coriander leaves
teaspoon of red/white wine vinegar
$^{1}/_{2}$ teaspoon of brown/muscovado sugar
juice of $^{1}/_{2}$ lime with grated zest
1 dessertspoon of olive oil
salt and freshly ground black pepper

Chop the tomatoes into smallish dice. Don't worry about skinning and de-seeding them (unless you really want to, of course). Place in a bowl with all the other ingredients except the coriander. Mix well and adjust the seasoning to taste. Chop the coriander and add to the mixed ingredients.

GREEN-FINGERED SHOPPING

You can easily banish growing pains with some canny green shopping to make sure you pick up the right basics for your green gardening:

The Organic Gardening Catalogue

This is the official catalogue of the Henry Doubleday Research Association (HDRA)—the UK's premier organic gardening organization. You can order anything from hollyhocks and spinach to strawberry plants and radishes, and some rare indigenous plants and vegetables which are supplied by Chase Organics. It's clear in the catalogue what is and isn't organic. You can also pick up a host of useful garden accessories to make your garden even greener, such as a water butt and rain saver or wooden composter. There's 10% discount on catalogue purchases for members of the HDRA.

Pay a visit to your local garden centre to see what's on offer. Many now have organic plant food and seed—but as usual you will need to check that it really is organic and not just green-sounding. Otherwise there is an abundance of mail order companies who can supply everything from 100% organic seeds to green gardening implements and materials. Some of these are listed in the Mini Directory.

If composting just seems too hands-on, and you don't fancy swapping recipes in a community scheme, you can always go out and buy some from the professionals. See the Mini Directory for some ideas of where to buy.

HELP & INSPIRATION

Many high-profile gardeners are organic enthusiasts, and there are a number of books on the subject. Check out organic-friendly gardeners, such as Monty Don, in weekend papers for weekly advice. Friends of the Earth and the Soil Association are also good places to find information and extra links (see Mini Directory for loads of other suggestions).

If you find your enthusiasm waning you can always try an away day to see some large scale professional organic gardens such as one of the Henry Doubleday Research Association's gardens round the country (details in Mini Directory). Ring or refer to the website to check opening times first.

living
la vida verde

So we've established that even our deeply urban lives can be enhanced by eating more natural food, and perhaps even growing the odd plant for ourselves. But what about the space in our homes? If we can't always exert our influence in the outside world, then this is the one place we should have ultimate control. However, almost all of our homes could benefit from a major green makeover.

SHUTTING OUT THE MEAN STREETS

Urban life can be dynamic, positively challenging and stimulating—but equally it can be exhausting, all-consuming and extremely stressful. Even the most banal of activities can become stressful in the face of traffic congestion, pollution, crowds and anti-social behaviour. In order to avoid complete burnout, we urbanites need some sort of time out every now and then, if only to cling to our sanity.

Finding space for some form of sanctuary where the madness stops for a few hours has of course become increasingly difficult. Despite a swelling population in the vast majority of urban areas, the number of green open spaces has declined. The pressure is on to work longer and longer hours, and spiralling costs mean that leisure activities have become more and more expensive. No surprise, then, that frazzled townies are increasingly prepared to channel their hard-earned cash into joining expensive health clubs, visiting holistic hangouts, and making frequent trips out of town.

Do you feel frazzled, frantic and frayed at the edges? Harness natural energy, fabrics and materials instead of chemicals in your home. Begin a green makeover to create a proper sanctuary that will give you some space away from the urban mean streets.

If we work it out properly, we should have access to a less expensive sanctuary: our homes. Our living space should provide a glorious respite from the mean streets. However, if you live in a major city your home is more likely to resemble a shoebox than the proverbial castle, but handled in the right way even the most spatially challenged living space should be able to offer a green haven of tranquillity in comparison to the chaos outside.

HOME TRUTHS

As a nation we have become home improvement fanatics, served by an endless stream of DIY and interior design pro-grammes, books and magazines. Sales of DIY products have boomed in recent years, as we spend one bank holiday after another buying everything from paint to tongue-and-groove panel-ing at home improvement super-stores, and spending some quality time on our living space.

Despite all this TLC, however, our homes are not the sanctuaries we might have hoped for. Although they might be cosmetically attractive, underneath the contemporary colour schemes and 'changing room' fea-tures lurk a host of allergens and potentially dangerous chemicals that could well be making us ill. From wall coverings and paints to low cost, trendy furniture, our interiors are filled with a concoction of synthetic chemicals that an increasing number of experts suggest are responsible for a range of unpleasant illnesses and symptoms, including headaches, skin and eye irritations, asthma, respiratory illnesses, allergies and nausea.

Aside from the thought that your living room could well contain enough chemicals to stock a small laboratory, there is also the problem of huge energy consumption. Our homes guzzle up an enormous amount of energy, and the average urban home is probably contributing more to global warming than the clapped-out old motor parked in the road outside. Household energy use accounts for a quarter of UK energy assumption—so turn that light off right now!

However, we're in the business of avoiding panic. A basic green makeover approached rationally can easily start to reverse the negative aspects in your home, and you can start the process of turning your home into a green sanctuary.

ALTERNATIVE TO ALLERGIES

Allergies on are on the increase. Symptoms that initially seem fairly innocuous can develop into debilitating conditions, including skin rashes, fatigue, headaches, and heightened sensitivity to all manner of substances. The response from many manufacturers is to introduce hypo-allergenic alternatives to everything from cosmetics to bedding. Unfortunately this often just means employing yet another set of chemicals to combat the original allergies, and can cause yet more damage to the immune system. Avoid jumping on the bandwagon, or being a martyr to your existing allergies, by steering clear of chemicals as far as possible and plumping for products which are truly natural.

MINI MAKEOVER: IMMEDIATE STEPS TO GREENING YOUR LIVING SPACE

LIGHTEN UP Open your home up to nature again, even on a small scale. Instead of immediately reaching for the light switch, open a curtain or the blinds and let some daylight in. Apart from saving energy, natural light can be an uplifting stimulus. Lighter window treatments such as voile and muslin can diffuse daylight into a room with designer effects. Obviously, you will have to switch on lights sometimes, but begin to replace conventional light bulbs with the low-energy version. They're cheaper in the long run too—they last longer.

CLUTTER BUSTER Shopaholics and hoarders take note: clutter is not a good look, and best confined to junk shops. Furniture manufacturers and designers have caught on to the fact that we are living in increasingly small areas yet continuing to buy even more stuff. They supply all manner of shelving units, clever cupboards and storage systems to control our possessions in small spaces. Although these undoubtedly have their uses, they are a way of bypassing the ultimate clutter buster: BUY LESS STUFF! New products appear on the market all the time, from gadgets to home accessories and everything in between. Many of them are not recyclable, and many give off nasty chemicals. Be more discerning— buy only what you need and what you really really want.

ZERO TOLERANCE for heavily packaged products that result in lots of litter. Read on for the low-down on recycling, but check out your local council's recycling scheme. Try to buy less (as above), and get used to separating products out. Recycling information (see Mini Directory) will tell you all you need to know.

EASY ALTERNATIVES Take advantage of whole new ranges of green household products, such as cream cleaners, disinfectants and toilet cleaners (see below), but you can also come up with some easy alternatives to unnecessary household products. Essential oils make brilliant, holistic air fresheners and they don't smell of fake pine forests and choke you in the process. Or you could try opening a couple of windows and getting some natural ventilation going.

SAVE YOUR ENERGY See Chapter 5 for more energy-saving hints, but start by incorporating some obvious energy-saving tactics into your normal routine. Turn lights off when you leave a room or when you really don't need them, only boil as much water as you need, turn appliances off when you're not using them, and question whether having a TV, computer and CD player on at the same time is really multi-tasking or just being wasteful.

INVEST IN RENEWABLE ENERGY Even if you're not in a position to harness the power of wind, water or solar energy immediately, or don't have the necessary funding for solar panels on your roof (or the space for wind turbines in your garden), you can look for a green energy supplier. A number of utility companies now offer a renewable energy package where you can either buy electricity that has been generated from a renewable source, or at least part of the cost per unit is channelled into a sustainable energy project. Unit Energy, endorsed by Friends of the Earth, is one such company (call 01249 705 550), but be prepared for costs being around 13–14% higher.

KEEP IT SIMPLE Simplicity is the key to a holistic, healthy green lifestyle. Aside from the health implications of toxic overload in the home, our psyche will benefit no end from a more natural and simple immediate environment. Even the most hardcore urban environment should have elements of natural simplicity.

AVOIDING TOXIC OVERLOAD

Continuing on our quest to be savvy green consumers, we need to wise up when it comes to shopping for the home. Bear in mind that cheap and cheerful furniture products are usually made from inferior, synthetic materials which can emit harmful vapours, and their lifespan isn't usually very long. The same may be true of electrical goods. Although you're not going to rush out to buy a new washing machine immediately, when you do replace your white goods make sure they're green. Opt for high quality goods that are likely to last, and buy on the basis of their water and energy efficiency. Efficient appliances used sparingly have a dramatic effect on decreasing energy consumption.

Some things to avoid and why:

MDF—the staple of any DIY programme, medium-density fibreboard actually contains formaldehyde and a combination of chemical adhesives. Formaldehyde is suspected by many to be a carcinogen, and it releases toxic vapours at room temperature.

Chipboard—also contains formaldehyde in the resin binder.

Petrochemical paints—which accounts for most commonly available paints. These contain Volatile Organic Compounds—don't be misled by the word 'organic', as VOCs include a wide range of compounds such as PVC (polyvinyl chloride) and PCB (polychlorinated biphenyls) which are highly toxic, and unsurprisingly have been related to a number of health problems.

Synthetic varnishes—these can trap chemicals in wood, which are then stored up and can be released when the surface becomes worn.

Carpets—not only can conventional carpets emit yet more formaldehyde vapours, but they can harbour dust mites that cause asthma and eczema. They are also stuck down with harmful adhesives.

Plastics—no longer hailed as fantastic, not only does plastic use up limited non-renewable oil reserves but it's a product of a mind-bogglingly energy-intensive process. Plastics aren't biodegradable, only a fraction of them can be recycled, and many forms emit potentially dangerous vapours.

MAXI MAKEOVER: LONG-TERM GREEN PLANS FOR YOUR HOME, FROM TOP TO BOTTOM

There are so many products now available that it is not difficult to find alternatives to decorate your home from top to bottom. From specialist companies with good product ranges to nationwide DIY giants, eco-friendly interiors have become big business. Next time your home needs to be redecorated, seize the opportunity to perform a green makeover. A holistic, healthy, inspiring and nurturing living space should be well within your grasp.

FLOORING

Kersaint Cobb flooring

Thankfully, the days of shag pile carpet in lairy colours are well behind us. Anything goes now, from wooden floors and rugs to stone flagging. However, many homes are still covered in synthetic fitted carpet which also provides a fine hideout and breeding ground for allergy-inducing carpet lice—however particular you may be with the hoover. Biodegradable, natural floorcovering is the perfect option, especially if you are prone to allergies. Originally, coir (scratchy and rather utilitarian) was the only option, but now many different materials and weaves are available. Materials such as jute can be quite soft, and herringbone designs look very smart. They also fit everywhere, from period properties to the very modern. Kersaint Cobb and Crucial Trading are two companies which have very good ranges.

TEXTILES

Just because cotton is from a plant doesn't mean that it is very eco-friendly; in fact the opposite is true. It's intensively farmed, sprayed with insecticides, and then to add insult to injury is normally chemically bleached and dyed. If you're houseproud and pushed for time, you may have been seduced by those 'easy iron' products—especially bed linen.

ABOVE: Stallholder showing that 'processed slices' are an anathema at farmer's markets.

BELOW: The only problem you'll encounter at Borough Market is being sidetracked by yet another great stall.

ABOVE: At Planet Organic, the rural backdrop makes the connection for us townies.

BELOW: Check out planet-fresh food— it's an entirely different experience.

CLOCKWISE FROM TOP LEFT:
The ultimate in convenience? Having your fresh, organic food delivered straight to your door / Cooking up a storm—Max and Sam at the Lavender Hill branch of Fresh and Wild.

The electric trike means you can always rely on a bit of assisted pedal power when you've just had enough of those hills.

Proving that harvest time comes to the most urban of vistas.

ABOVE: The contemporary look—wood with natural paints and varnishes from Green Building Store.

BELOW: Natural Collection's salt crystal lamps and recycled glassware give an atmospheric touch to an eco-interior.

Inside and out – ABOVE: an inspirational glimpse of the dream green home.
BELOW: Contemporary bamboo furniture from Weiming, illustrating that
the words 'natural' and 'stylish' are no longer strangers.

There are ample opportunities to demonstrate your eco-enthusiasm through some green gifts: from cosmetics to children's toys, they're all covered.

But (surprise, surprise) these are covered in chemicals. Organic cotton might not be wrinkle-free, but it will be GM- and chemical-free. If you don't fancy doing lots of ironing, rest assured that eco-chic is supposed to look natural too!

Texture is big news in interiors, and luckily that is one quality that truly natural products have in abundance. Hemp is a great alternative to cotton, is hardy enough to grow without any fertilizers, and grows prolifically. Even non-organic hemp is environmentally sound. If this is one hippie move too far, don't be nervous: the production of hemp is now licensed, and you don't have to be a Woodstock throwback to make use of it. Silk is also a good interiors option, though it is expensive. Make sure it's from a recognized, ethically sound importer. Flannel, flax and felt, while they may not sound like the sexiest fabrics in the world, are often chemical-free and are experiencing a bit of a renaissance—they've even been used on walls!

INSULATE

Yes, in true Blue Peter style get those draught excluders out and fill up the holes and cracks where your heat is escaping. If you were under the impression that loft insulation was only something your dad was interested in, think again! If your loft is insulated properly (insulation needs to be 20 cm thick to be truly effective) then you can save around 20 per cent of your heating costs. If you're in a shared house, or in a flat within a shared house, make sure that whoever is responsible for the loft has it insulated properly. Get an eco-friendly brand such as Warmcel by Filcrete (which is made from recycled newspaper, and once it's outlived its purpose insulating your loft it can be recycled again). You can save even more dosh by ensuring that your water cylinder is wrapped up properly.

PERFECT PAINTS

Conventional paints include a host of allergy-inducing chemicals, from solvents to synthetic resins. In particular, oil-based paints are full of solvents which contribute to air pollution. Try to use a latex, water-based paint if you can only get hold of normal paint, but there are plenty of companies now which provide green or organic paint using natural substances like beeswax. Auro is one such company that offers a comprehensive range of paints and colours; they will even do specialized tests for people who suffer from a range of allergies which might be triggered by natural substances as well as chemical compounds.

VINTAGE IS COOL

Retro chic is not only big news in fashion, it's huge in interiors! Modern re-takes just don't have the appeal of some of the originals, so you might as well join the cognoscenti and scour junk shops and second-hand stores for chairs, mirrors and all manner of goodies to deck out your home. Unusually for a trend, this way of recycling is a real environmental plus. Salvage yards are full of rich pickings, if you are doing up your home. Situated all over the country, you will find everything from water troughs to 50s kitchen cupboards and groovy radiators. They are a green and inventive way of finding the perfect look for your living space. You can swot up on the ways of salvage yards on the web at <www.salvo.co.uk>.

WHY WOOD IS GOOD

Provided that furniture is not made from so-called jungle wood—tropical hardwoods, which are extremely precious and environmentally vital—wood is a great natural and renewable source. Again, you need to be sure that it has not been treated with any chemical substances: wooden floorboards should only be treated with natural products like beeswax.

THE FULL MONTY

How far you take your green makeover will depend on a variety of different factors: when you're next decorating, how involved you want to become, and what resources you have available (usually money and time). If you become deeply committed to the prospect of living in an eco-home, you might end up considering everything from solar power to a compost toilet. Of course, in an urban environment where there is little space, there is less opportunity to transform a conventional property into a eco-home unless the building is a new one or part of a new initiative (see Focus on BedZED at the end of this chapter).

If you aren't building from scratch, you can always check out some eco-options to see what you can incorporate into your current home. Because of increasing demand, it's getting cheaper to manufacture solar panels, and even design luminaries like Paul Smith have become involved as they become the ultimate accessory. Jeremy Leggett is a high profile proponent of the mighty powers of solar energy, so check out <www.solar-century.co.uk> to see if you could convert your home—it might well be easier than you think. You can even get DIY solar water-heating systems from some manufacturers, as the technology is quite simple. But if you like to get the professionals in, remember to get quotes as you would with any building or maintenance job. Just because you're being environmentally friendly, there's no need to pay over the odds.

See the Mini Directory for further contacts for an eco-home.

LIVING AWAY FROM HOME

If you rent your living space or live in other accommodation such as halls of residence, you'll have less control over your surroundings and immediate environment. Try and specify that your accommodation is as eco-friendly as possibly, especially if it is being kitted out or redecorated before you move in. If you are limited to small gestures, buy a couple of organic house plants to help to detoxify the space, and make sure there is plenty of ventilation. Make sure you or the person responsible for cleaning uses green products, and make any allergies known.

KIT OUT YOUR GREEN HOME

Lots of companies now sell green products for the home. From recycled glassware to environmentally friendly pillows, you should be able to find what you're looking for—if not in your local high street, where the options are generally still quite poor, then by mail order or internet sites. See the Mini Directory for companies that have a good selection.

GREEN CLEAN

Domestic duties may not be particularly scintillating, but they represent big business for huge companies and their marketing teams who want to persuade us that we can't live without their particular brand of toilet cleaner or washing powder. But yes, you've guessed it: the bulk of these wondrous substances which will free us from domestic drudgery in under three minutes are actually heady concoctions of toxic chemicals which could well affect more than your surfaces. Even if they don't trigger allergic reactions in us, they contain all manner of compounds which are not biodegradable or slow to biodegrade, and which enter straight into our water supply and do untold ecological damage.

LAUNDRY TIPS

If you can't get a green brand of washing powder, go for a conventional concentrated powder rather than a liquid. Make sure you have a full load before you wash. Putting a wash on for one pair of socks and a T-shirt is a no-no.

THE BIG CLEAN-UP

Green cleaning products use biodegradable, natural ingredients which have the minimum ecological impact possible. You'll need to try and test a few brands, but most of them are as effective as conventional products. Because they don't have optical brighteners, colorants and artificial fragrances, they can seem a bit strange at first—but have faith! Your clothes are still clean, they just won't smell so synthetic! Until you're sure which makes are best for you, you'll need to employ those label skills and check out the small print. You're looking for cleaners and washing powders based on vegetable rather than petrochemical ingredients. As a rule of thumb, if you recognize most of the ingredients, then you're on the right track, but if it reads like a chemistry set give it a miss.

Substances to avoid in cleaners:

Phenols: found in plastics and disinfectants as well as in paints and varnishes. They are carbolic acids and suspected of causing damage to the respiratory system.

Organochlorines: found in many cleaners and air fresheners. Contain a mixture of unwelcome substances, including chloroform and chloramines. Suspected of causing skin irritation, fatigue, depression and headaches.

Ecover produce a good range of products for every corner of your home. They're stocked all over the country, and even in many supermarkets. When you've finished a product you can earn extra brownie points by refilling your bottles. Quite a few specialist organic and green stores across the country stock the giant vats of Ecover cleaning fluids from which you can refill your empties. If you really want to know what goes into your cleaning products you could always try a few DIY products and keep them in clearly marked, recycled containers.

Cure-all cleaner:

> $1/2$ cup bicarbonate of soda
> organic liquid soap solution
> $1/2$ cup vinegar

Mix everything together in your cleaning cauldron. You can then add 6–10 drops of organic tea tree oil or grapefruit seed extract (both antibacterial substances) followed by 6 drops of essential oil (lemon provides a clean, fresh smell) to get rid of any nasty niffs. This is a good substitute for any all-purpose cleaner.

Bathroom Blaster

Mix together $1/2$ cup baking soda and $1/2$ cup white vinegar, add a few drops of lemon essential oil, a few drops of tea tree oil and some warm water, and then you can blitz those tiles, sink and loo until they shine.

Fridge Freshener

A pungent-smelling fridge is particularly revolting, so leave an open box of bicarbonate of soda with a couple of drops of our favourite lemon essential and tea tree oils in there. Make sure it's clearly marked as something that's not to be eaten, just in case there's any late night, post-pub confusion, for example.

Drain Dodger

Pour $1/2$ cup of baking soda down the drain, quickly followed by $1/2$ cup of vinegar. Leave it for about quarter of an hour and then set to work with hot water and a plunger to get everything flowing smoothly.

Rug Renaissance

Sprinkle a thin layer of baking soda on the rug or carpet in question, and allow it to sit for about 30 minutes (making sure that nobody takes this opportunity to walk over the area). Then hoover away all the grime.

Whiter than white

Are your whites are looking a bit tired, or on the grey side? Use $1/2$ cup of white vinegar, baking soda or borax per normal wash load to help perk them up.

focus on bedzed

A revolutionary new housing project in South London using solar power and electric cars offers urbanites a new way of living. . . .

On the site of a former sewage works in South London, the BedZED housing project has transcended the less than auspicious past of this brownfield area to become a cutting edge environmental, eco-chic hous-

ing project. BedZED is a solar urban village in Beddington which has been designed to provide low-cost housing and work space. The generation of heat and power is carbon neutral, meaning that it does not add to the amount of carbon dioxide already in the atmosphere.

There are 82 BedZED properties for rent and sale, as well as 1600 square metres of workspace and a large sports facility. The Peabody Trust, a London housing charity, has developed BedZED for low-cost, affordable housing. Adrian Pancucci, spokesman for the Peabody Trust, points out the appeal: "BedZED attracts buyers with an interest in environmental issues and people who are simply looking for a place to live in this area."

photo credit © BP plc (2001)

Innovations abound on this project, beginning with an 108-kilowatt photovoltaic (PV) system at the site, which also has a combined heat and power plant which uses waste wood from sustainable forestry for fuel. BedZED's designer, Bill Dunster, explains it simply: "We've reduced the energy requirement for providing heat and power. This means that renewable energy becomes a viable option."

As the buildings are super-insulated, the biggest loss of heat is from ventilation. A wind-driven ventilation system uses outgoing stale air to

*warm up incoming fresh air. A living roof of sedum—a perennial plant—
also serves as insulation.*

*The BedZED project has also used 1,138 solar panels, which gener-
ate power and provide the 'skin' of the building. The design of the panels has been quite a challenge. Mounted on south-facing walls, vertical
panels are made to fit standard window frames that can be installed by
glazers, without requiring them to have any specialist knowledge of PV
systems. The idea is to get builders familiar with working with environmental initiatives and demonstrate that it can be a very ordinary part of
the building.*

*Energy demand in BedZED homes will be about 25% of the amount
of a conventional building of the same size. As Bill Dunster points out,
"It is essential that we get demand down by increasing energy efficiency
if the use of PV is to have any significance at all."*

*As an extra, eco-sensitive BedZED residents can buy electric cars at
subsidized prices. Electricity generated from the site's PV systems is supplied from charging points at parking spaces around the development.
The fuel cost is much less than for conventional vehicles, and enough
power is generated from the PV systems to charge 40 cars which users
are encourage to share in a car pool scheme.*

Visit the website at <www.bedzed.org.uk>.

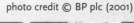

photo credit © BP plc (2001)

eco-chic
comes to town

WHY GREEN CAN BE THE NEW BLACK

Until recently, the term 'eco-style' might have been considered something of a contradiction. Traditionally, 'greenies' have committed a wide variety of fashion *faux pas*, from wearing socks with sandals and billowing tie-dye trousers, to shapeless knitted sweaters in rainbow colours. It's not an image that's had popular appeal—particularly in cosmopolitan hubs, where the sartorial stakes are higher. But something began to change: Birkenstocks became fashionable, eco-designers raised their game, and a whole new audience has discovered green chic.

Clothes stores are now filled with synthetic fibres which are developed to 'perform' under a whole host of extreme conditions. Admittedly our weather may be varied, but it is rarely extreme, and in our daily lives it is not altogether apparent why we need such high performance outfits. So-called innovative, millennium materials are increasingly being used for high fashion, but the results cannot always be predicted—a top jeans manufacturer was forced to recall thousands of pairs of a new range because they produced toxic emissions when ironed.

Taking an overview of the textile industry, you would be forced to conclude that it is an ecological nightmare, with cotton production topping the charts as the world's most polluting crop. But fortunately we have the opportunity to exercise responsible consumer power by trying out some natural fashion in the form of non-adulterated, ethically produced materials. An expanding array of specialists, and an increased awareness of the importance of well-designed clothes, means that green fashion needn't represent a fashion disaster.

In the past, 'green' design pretty much began and ended with wind chimes, a hessian bean bag and a couple of joss-sticks. These days the materials might be natural, but the design is distinctly contemporary.

BEAUTY MYTH AND BEAUTY FACT

It takes a supremely self-assured girl to stick with the old soap and water routine. Let's be honest, most of us are tempted by products galore for every type of look and every cosmetic eventuality. And boys should watch out too: the male cosmetic industry is increasingly big business, as the male of the species is finally persuaded to tone and moisturize. Preening and painting has become part of the daily routine for most of us, and one we love. We urbanites can even buy products that form a barrier to pollution. However, what is not always apparent is that many of these potions contain less than wholesome ingredients, and may actually be doing more harm than good.

Worryingly, a manufacturer only need have a small fraction of natural ingredients or substances derived from a natural plant to be labelled 'natural'. So remember that quasi-green names and logos and stylish packaging featuring mother earth colours mean absolutely nothing. Around 100,000 tonnes of man-made chemicals find their way into cosmetics which are labelled as 'natural'. It is estimated that women absorb up to two kilograms of chemicals per year through toiletries and cosmetics, so it's about time we gave some deep thought to what exactly goes into these products.

The solution is to use products which are truly natural, and fortunately there are a number of well respected brands around that can provide green alternatives for most of your essential products, and for some frivolous ones besides. Good green shops or specialist stores such as Fresh & Wild will have a good range, and you might even find green products in conventional chemists. Alternatively, try some internet or mail order shopping (<www.ecozone.co.uk>, tel: 020 8777 3121 and <www.ThinkNatural.com>, tel: 0845 6011223 have good ranges). As with cleaning products, a genuinely organic or green product will not have an ingredients list that reads like a chemistry set. Many will also be certified. Check the ingredients carefully and look for natural products such as essential oils, herbs, olive oil, rose water and sea salts.

SOME TOP PROVIDERS FOR URBAN BEAUTY AND THEIR BIGGEST HITS

Weleda has 40 years expertise in creating chemical-free health and beauty products. Based on a true understanding and knowledge of plants and their

properties, Weleda products are widely available, highly effective and smell fantastic. They also have a good range for men.

• BEST BUYS: Iris Facial Toner, Iris Moisture Cream, Calendula Toothpaste, Rosemary Milk Bath.

Dr Hauschka: developed during the 1950s, the range uses bio-dynamically or organically grown herbs and plants from their head-quarters in Germany, grown on approved farms or in wild areas which are environmentally secure, and gathered by hand just before sunrise!

• BEST BUYS: foundations, lip balm, rejuvenating mask.

Green People: a host of products manufactured to high standards, using organically grown herbs and plants wherever possible, or material collected responsibly from wild stocks.

• BEST BUYS: Happy Kids Range with everything from toothpaste to shower gel for groovy green kids; Edelweiss Sun Lotion SPF 15.

Faith in Nature began in 1974. A large range of skin, hair and bodycare products are made with 100% nat-ural essential oils in a biodegradable vegetable base. They contain no artificial colour, fragrances, animal products or petrochemicals.

• BEST BUYS: Tea Tree Bath and Shower Gel, Aloe Conditioner.

Napiers Herbalists Napiers Dispensary was established in 1860 by Duncan Napier, and many of the products which are available by mail order are based on his original recipes.

BEST BUYS: Buy the basics to make your own completely personal cosmetics: Beeswax, Rose Petals and Vegan Base Cream.

Neal's Yard Remedies: These well known little blue bottles and jars have been coming out of the original Covent Garden store since 1981. NYR products are now stocked all over the place, and they also have a thriving mail order business. Neal's Yard are committed to helping us discover our potential "energy, health and wisdom".

• BEST BUYS: So divine are many of the NYR products that it's hard to single out any, and nearly impossible to pick a dud. The Elderflower Hand Softener is bordering on heavenly, and the Calendula Cleanser also has an awesome reputation. Their travel accessories are handy, and there are not many people on this planet who would say no to one of their gift boxes.

BEAUTY TIPS TO SHAKE OFF
THE GRIME AND GRIT OF THE CITY

Give your skin condition an extra boost by brushing regularly with a natural fibre body brush. Forget antiperspirants: they pollute the environment and could well have serious health implications (scientists are

investigating a link between spray-on deodorants and cases of breast cancer). But if you've ever been on any form of public transport during rush hour in the summer, you'll understand why going *au naturelle* is not a very public-spirited move: deodorant stones are available by mail order and in most green stores and shops; or skincare specialists such as Weleda produce their own, effective and natural spray-on.

Shun extravagantly packaged moisturizers, no matter what amazing attributes they boast. All style and chemicals, and very little substance—you're better off reaching for a trusty bottle of organic olive oil. A couple of lidfuls in the bath will soften up your skin no end.

Use olive oil again to pamper your stressed-out, polluted, frazzled tresses. Wash your hair with an eco-shampoo and follow with a green conditioner or a small amount of olive oil or whipped organic eggs for an intensive conditioning treatment. Make sure you wash it out thoroughly. Old food in hair is not a good look.

Treat split ends to a honey treatment. Mix 1 tsp Honey with 2 tbsps olive oil, then beat in an egg yolk. Massage on to your hair in small sections. Wait for 30 minutes. Rinse and shampoo.

Pre-empt allergies by doing a patch test to try out any new products. Apply a small amount of the new substance on to the inside of your wrist, cover and leave over night. If any irritation occurs you'll know before it's too late that you're sensitive to the product or some of the ingredients.

GREEN GIFTS

In order to maintain a meaningful urban existence and relationships with our fellow urbanites, it's a good idea not to become too worthy. Embracing an eco-friendly lifestyle without being too 'holier than thou' can be a difficult path to tread, but a constructive, softly softly approach shouldn't scare off your nearest and dearest. Nor do you have to abandon your old instincts completely. Take shopping for example. Whilst environmentally we need to cut down on the volume of purchases and buying four things when one will do, there is still room for some green retail therapy.

Searching out green gifts gives you a good opportunity to exercise your discerning consumer habits alongside your new improved eco-friendly habits. Christmas, birthdays and anniversaries present the ideal opportunity to employ some creative thinking, exercise your eco-knowledge and your green consumer vote.

Clever cosmetics for boys and girls

Plus points: you can put together your own collection of green lotions and potions tailored for the recipient. You can also sidestep paying for the unnecessary packaging and branding which comes with the usual suspects.

Minus points: You can't just give someone a collection of bottles and bars of soap, so you'll need to use your creative/Blue Peter talents and put together an attractive box yourself. Reuse a box, cover in some decorative natural, recycled paper and fill in the gaps with some paper shreddings.

Overall score: 8/10. Although this doesn't score full marks for originality, it does enable you to introduce your nearest and dearest to your favourite holistic products and you can choose things specially to give that individual touch.

Spiritual Fancies
Feng shui incense sticks, meditation music.

Plus points: these will undoubtedly de-stress even the most uptight of your friends.

Minus points: not everybody is comfortable with chanting and chilling out.

Overall score: 6/10. Nice idea, but might suggest you have developed hippy-dippy tendencies and invite suggestions of stereotypical eco-behaviour.

Gardening Gear

Plus points: there are many for whom gardening is not just a hobby but an obsession. Such green-fingered friends and relatives will like nothing better than a horticulturally-inspired present. You can choose from the deeply practical (organic growing powder and foliar spray) to the more frivolous (solar fountains and globe lights).

Minus points: if this is a gift for someone very close to you, encouraging them to spend even more time outdoors may mean you see even less of them.

Overall score: 9/10. An excellent idea to inspire and encourage everyone to get really green in the garden.

Healthy Hampers

Plus points: you can't often go wrong with some carefully selected and arranged delicacies, and there are plenty of organic alternatives to choose from. Foodstuffs from porcini to relishes look good in a nice natural hamper that can then be utilized for organic picnics. For that extra sparkle, you can even throw in a bottle of organic champagne (read on to Chapter 6 for some facts about organic booze). If you don't want to trail round selecting your own organic ingredients, you can buy a variety of ready-made hampers.

Minus points: unlike conventional food, organic alternatives aren't chock-full of preservatives, so you'll need to ensure your hamper is made up of things that are going to last.

Overall score: 8/10. Foodies will love it, but make sure it looks stylish and steer away from that harvest festival vibe.

Things for little people

Plus points: there are fantastic children's toys and games made from natural fibres and materials. It's no longer just the traditional farm sets and rag dolls that you can find from green manufacturers. There's a whole host of push along, sit along toys, dolls' furniture, board games and accessories. It's also much more reassuring to give small children toxic-free soft toys.

Minus points: Your green toys have to be pretty imaginative to compete with global, high tech ones in lurid plastics.

Overall score: 9/10. It's good to get kids handling natural materials and helps them use their finely tuned imaginations.

For the Gadget Obsessed

Plus points: there's nothing your average gadget nerd likes better than to introduce a new object into the household. What better than a green gadget with eco-benefits, rather than a useless piece of plastic that will be discarded after five minutes.

Minus points: Some of these gifts may be slightly lacking in glamour, but then again your average gadget freak won't really care.

Overall score: 8/10. Scores low on the luxurious pampering rating, but gadgets such as a potato clock have innovative appeal and a solar radio is definitely useful.

Scratchy hand knitted socks in a bright colour

Plus points: making these by hand shows some effort and provided the wool has been dyed and treated naturally you've shown good commitment to the green cause by using a natural, renewable material.

Minus points: giving someone socks suggests a lack of imagination and creativity, and no one likes uncomfortable, bulky socks in any case.

Overall score: 0/10. This present bypasses all eco-chic possibilities, and will only convince everybody that you are a loopy tree-hugger.

See the Mini Directory for some stockist ideas.

diary: the domestic challenge

The prospect of guests arriving at our humble abode always fills me with horror because it highlights just how humble our abode actually is. There can be no denying that our spatially challenged flat is filled with unnecessary stuff (as Ben likes to point out, most of it is mine), so it's rather an uphill struggle to keep it in any kind of order.

At the moment our bathroom is doing a very convincing impression of a well-stocked pharmacy. Restricted shelf space is filled with half-full bottles, tubs and jars of various potions and lotions. Sadly, I seem to lack any kind of resistance when it comes to buying stuff that promises to make my hair shinier, teeth whiter or eyelashes longer.

Close inspection of a number of the miracle products on my bathroom shelves has revealed that many of the ingredients are not as wholesome as I would have hoped. In fact the majority of them just read like a long list of chemicals, featuring delights such as polyethylene glycol or methylparaben, and I don't like the idea of these coming into direct contact with my skin. Ben points out that the same problems apply to many of our household staples. All of our conventional laundry and cleaning products include chemicals that we would rather not unleash on either our immediate or surrounding environment.

I launch a two-pronged attack on a) the quantity of stuff I have bought which I don't need, and b) the chemical infusions that up until now I have insisted on buying in so many forms. The first step is to have a big clear-out. Rather than throwing everything out, I opt for a well-known form of recycling—the car boot sale, which will also make us some extra cash as well. A quick scan of the local paper reveals five car boot sales on a Sunday morning, all in the surrounding area. And no, you don't even need a car—so we conscript a friend, Annie, who also has some stuff to get rid of, and head down with two large bags of stuff and a small trestle table. Obviously this form of recycling only works if you don't immediately run out and buy new stuff to replace the old. We get rid of almost everything, from last month's magazines to bottles of bubble bath and old textiles that we don't have room for. It's amazing what you can find at a car boot sale. But remember, nobody is going to pay high prices for things, so you won't get rid of many high quality, pricey items.

While the car boot sale has got rid of much of the debris, it's important to maintain this good work. I've noticed a number of charity shops which collect old furniture, as well as organizations that deal specifically with old curtains and other large pieces of fabric in a kind of fabric exchange. As a self-confessed shopaholic and hoarder, it's taking a serious effort to stop me accumulating more stuff. I have come up with an effective process of demystifying the objects that I think I want to buy, which takes out the compulsive element! First of all, with cosmetics and toiletries I read the ingredients. This

—— diary ——

is very effective, as after this, the glamorous box or bottle doesn't seem half so appealing. With other products I have also taken to analysing the packaging, and with those items that are wrapped in yet more plastic, visualizing them in a vast landfill site. I also try to remember that 'recyclable' doesn't mean that it necessarily will be.

Where we need to replace products, we are opting for green alternatives. As something of a connoisseur of bodycare products and cosmetics, I am fairly impressed by the range of eco-alternatives, though admittedly the ranges in conventional stores and supermarkets are fairly unimpressive. Many of the vegetable soaps, organic facial toner and moisturizers definitely give their conventional counterparts a run for their money. However, we did experience a completely disgusting organic toothpaste. Ben and I were really unimpressed by this brown gel version, which made us want to book emergency appointments with the nearest dental hygenist. Forced to chuck this version, we have been brave enough to give another 'green' version a try: we're finding Weleda's Calendula toothpaste effective, and it tastes quite pleasant too!

Even though we had a bunch of normal cleaning products, we've replaced these with green cleaners, mostly from Ecover. We were keen to get rid of the chemical versions as soon as possible, and to see what the alternatives are like. The washing-up liquid seems just as good, and the disinfectant substitute has a rather nice citrus smell. The all-purpose cream cleaner cleans the bath well with a bit of elbow grease, but does require more rinsing than the usual cleaner to remove a white sediment that really shows up. Slightly more effort than usual, but at least we've got some piece of mind.

Even a flat as small as ours seems to need constant attention, so we're always in the process of decorating. In the spirit of keeping it green, I've ordered some organic paint samples and swatches of natural floorcovering. We're not quite ready for a solar roof and a compost toilet, but at least it's a step in the right direction. I'm under no illusion—we're not going to create an eco-home overnight (especially with our limited budget), but I'm really keen to bring in some changes, especially as I do have mild allergies which I would like to bring under control.

Chapter 6

green
scene

However green you manage to make your urban lifestyle, it is still unlikely that you will be tucked up amongst your eco-friendly sheets with a mug of organic cocoa listening to a wind-up radio by 9 pm. Going out, whether mooching around coffee bars during the day or living it up well after the sun goes down, is an integral part of most peoples' urban experience. So the question is: how green can you get in your leisure time, and what sort of places are there to hang out? From Glasgow to Plymouth, the green scene is gathering pace and giving us the opportunity to go out without shelving our green lifestyles. In town after town, it's getting easier to sink an organic pint on a Friday night—and avoiding a concoction of allergy-inducing chemicals might mean that you can avoid some of those stupefying hangovers.

HEALTH-UNCONSCIOUS ORGANICS

Whilst there are obviously major benefits to many green or organic products, it's worth remembering that whilst eco-cigs might be produced more ethically and be less full of chemicals than conventional cigarettes, that doesn't negate the potentially harmful effects. Nor is organic booze going to be alright if you're not supposed to drink. Whilst it doesn't contain a concoction of chemicals, it's still alcoholic.

If you are a vegan, remember also that organic wines are not always vegan or vegetarian. When the wine is being cleared of residue—known as the fining process—egg whites, casein (a milk protein) and isinglass (derived from fish) may have been used. Vegan or vegetarian wines use betonite clay as a fining agent, or leave the wine to clear naturally. Vegan

Good news – green doesn't have to equal virtuous! Fortunately there's a whole array of distractions when it comes to living it up green-style.

wines should be clearly marked, and these are the ones you need to choose in order to be sure no animal products have been used.

THE LO-DOWN ON DRINKING ORGANIC

If you're afraid of becoming too worthy, fear not! A booming organic booze industry means that you don't have to give up behaving disgracefully just yet. A demand for green alcohol, other than crème de menthe, means that you can now get your paws on everything from organic spirits, beers and ales to wine—all chemical-free.

WHY ORGANIC WINE?

If you still have an image of wine-making as a wholesome cottage industry where ruddy-cheeked grape-pickers crush the crop underneath their feet, then you need to know the truth! Vast vineyards have taken over the landscape in many countries, and destroyed a substantial amount of wildlife. Chemicals are used liberally, and most normal vineyards are sprayed with fertilizers, pesticides and fungicides several times before harvest. The problem is particularly pertinent in developing countries where wine is now being produced for the first time. Without any tradition of winemaking, or the reputation and prestige which comes with the tradition, new wine countries use price points to undercut the competition and make an entrance on to the retailer's shelves. In too many incidences, widespread use of pesticides has been linked to the devastating health problems experienced by the low-paid pickers on vineyards. Practices like these might bring the price of wine down in supermarkets and off licences by a few pence, but they also continue the cycle of abuse of both workers and the environment.

By contrast, organic wines are produced from grapes grown to strict guidelines in order that they can be certified. Chemical fertilizers and pesticides are prohibited, and only very low sulphur levels are permitted.

WHY ORGANIC WINE IS
SUCH GOOD NEWS

Organic wine growers use organic fertilizers such as seaweed and natural composts—these nourish the soil rather than pollute it.

Nitrogen-fixing plants are grown between the vines, and 'good' insects are introduced to combat all the vine-loving pests—natural pest control. Synthetic yeast cultures are dispensed with in the wine-making process: instead, natural yeasts which form on the bloom of the grapes are used in fermentation.

Conventional wine production uses large quantities of sulphur dioxide to sterilize and preserve. Organic wines only use very small quantities, or none at all.

Organic wine should be certified. The vineyards have to be checked and approved by certification bodies, and there are on-site checks to ensure that the appropriate standards are being met. As many of the wines are imported—the bulk are from France—you need to check the labelling carefully.

BIODYNAMIC WINE

If you want to make doubly sure that you are imbibing a chemical-free wine and one that's been made in harmony with the environment, try biodynamic wines. In common with biodynamic farming practices for growing food (see Chapter 2, Go Wild With Food), wine production follows the practices defined by Rudolph Steiner, using a holistic style of agriculture, to create harmony between plant, soil, moon and planets.

Biodynamic growers give their wines the best possible start by planting their vineyards near the time of the new moon. The reasoning behind this is that it's the time when the earth's gravitational rhythms are downwards, the same direction that the baby vine's roots need to go if it is to prosper.

BD wines are made from 100% biodynamically grown grapes, meaning that the grapes have not been subjected to pesticides, herbicides, fungicides, chemical fertilizers, or synthetic chemicals of any kind either on the vines or in the soil.

Connoisseurs claim that biodynamic wines (and organic wines in general) reveal their true flavours, as the true flavour of the grape is not masked by chemicals.

No added sulphites are used, which is a big bonus for anyone who suffers from allergic reactions.

Top Tipples:

If you can't find a good selection of organic or biodynamic wines nearby, you can still revel in the green drink revolution by joining an organic wine club.

•   Try The Organic Wine Club, 261 Upper Town Street, Leeds LS13 3JT. Tel: 0113 257 7545.

GREEN BEER

The British are known, not always in a positive sense, for their connection with beer. Organic beer is a growing trend, especially in the UK: even hardened beer drinkers have commented on its superior taste, without accounting for the positive eco-effects. In the last ten years, the brewing industry in the UK has essentially passed into the hand of a few multinational companies. This means mass production and cost-cutting, and the result in many cases has been to reduce natural ingredients in favour of synthetic, low cost substitutes. However, fans of beer are not easily fooled, and smaller-scale operations offering naturally produced beer are coming up trumps.

I AM A CIDER DRINKER

Don't think that as an organic drinker you are limited to wine and beer. There are now organic alternatives for all kind of liquor, including vodka and gin. Often overlooked, and perhaps due for something of a renaissance, is cider. There are hundreds of kinds of indigenous apples in the UK, many of which are now grown organically, and therefore not surprisingly there's a huge tradition of cider-making here. Traditional cider makers who do a good range of organic varieties are increasingly in evidence at city farmers' markets.

PUKKA TUKKA AND THE JUICE REVOLUTION

Drinking culture can be a major part of our social lives, but it's not the only time we go out to see and be seen. No longer are we content to spend solitary lunchtimes at our desks with soggy sandwiches produced from Tupperware containers. We now require daily distractions other than the traditional pub, whether breaking our shopping schedule for a coffee or popping out of the office for lunch with some friends. Café society has emerged on pavements all over the UK, and these are increasingly of the green variety. You'll find at least a couple of organic or green restaurants and cafés in most town centres. Their green credentials are usually quite explicit, but you should be able to tell from the menu whether or not they are organic, vegan, or merely use wholemeal bread. Don't be afraid to ask questions.

If you despair of ever kicking your coffee habit, you could try catching on to the juice bar craze and head down to one of these—an alternative to traditional coffee bars and the rather outdated tea shops. Springing up in many town centres, in sections of organic stores and in the corner of health clubs, the juice bar is bringing a small taste of California to our British palates. Many use organic, seasonal fruit squeezed before your eyes and mixed into delicious cocktails. Not only will you get your much needed dose of vitamins and minerals, but you can also experience the unexpected delights of combinations such as beetroot and apple.

The increasing number of organic restaurants means that those who like good food but don't want to compromise their commitment to eating fresh, unadulterated produce are well served in a number of cities. Quite a few top chefs have adopted the organic cause, which is hardly surprising as these are the very people who are passionate about the state of food and the taste of good quality fresh produce. It can still be difficult to find totally organic menus in some places, and many restaurants serve a mix of organic and conventional. However, this will change as organic goods become easier to source and as more kitchens change to a totally organic system. In those establishments who have made the change, you'll find every level of eating out is catered for, from the easy, informal food in organic gastro-pubs up to the top restaurants.

focus: the freedom brewing company

One company that has been winning the taste wars and proving the power of naturally produced beer is the Freedom Brewing Company. Launched in 1995, Freedom became the first dedicated microbrewer of lager in the UK. Operating on the simple premise that the fresher beer is, the better it tastes, the company produces beer in strict accordance with the Reinheitsgebot (German purity laws dating from 1516), and only uses the best natural ingredients.

The basic concept is that a talented master brewer can make varied flavours out of four essential and unvarying pure ingredients—water, malted barley, hops and yeast. If it sounds simple, it is. But this is no archaic operation: despite the fact the beer is brewed according to guidelines established in the 16th Century, two cutting edge bars (Freedom micro-brew bars) in central London highlight the company's contemporary appeal.

If you can't make it to soak up both the beer and the atmosphere in the London bars, don't despair! Freedom Organic Pilsner (certified by the Soil Association) and other Freedom beers free from additives and preservatives are available in bars and off licences all over the country. You can also indulge if you are a vegan, as all the beers are filtered, not fined.

focus on org:
why lucky leeds is singing
the praises of org

ORG is the brainchild of Novita and Wai-Vii, who came up with the idea for a happening organic hang-out independently when they were both studying at Leeds. After graduating, they got together and decided to give it a go: ORG opened its doors in August 2000. They cannily chose Leeds after seeing how the green scene had developed in the south-east, and recognizing the potential of Leeds to become the trend capital of the North. "We wanted to offer the North the same opportunity to experience the organic revolution—Leeds is one the fastest growing cities in the UK, and closely follows the trends of London, as demonstrated by the fact that it has its own Harvey Nichols store," explains Wai-Vii. They chose a location slap bang in the city centre, and set out to be a comprehensive resource for green products, as well as a trendy juice bar and meeting place for the bright young things of Leeds. Both girls have a long-held interest in organic living—not just eating organic, but a more holistic approach to life, particularly city life.

So, lucky Leeds! ORG offers a cool, new shopping experience, award-winning products which up until now have only really been available in London, and a funky, well-designed juice bar where customers can hang out and keep themselves informed about a dynamic green community. Hardly surprising, then, that ORG is a mecca for all kinds of people including mothers, students and professionals.

Chapter 7

nitty gritty
eco-living

So we've addressed some of the finer points of an eco-lifestyle: shopping around for green cosmetics, flicking through green mail order catalogues, floating around farmers' markets picking up fresh produce, and indulging in a spot of green interior design. All fabulous and in the right direction, but it's also time to look at a couple of fundamental features to underpin our greener lifestyle. Waste reduction and disposal is not really up there in the glamour stakes with holistic healing and yoga classes, but it is nevertheless a vital part of the green experience.

Once we've sorted out our own immediate environment, it's probably a good time to work out how we should travel to other peoples'. And the answer, as you may suspect, should be in the most ecologically unobtrusive and least destructive way. The second half of this chapter is dedicated to travel, the problems of our current vehicle-centred lives, how to minimize the damage, and some possible alternatives.

AN ECO-TIP

Urbanites can again hang their heads in shame—we are particularly guilty when it comes to disposable living. We are hot-headed consumers, compulsively buying and then almost instantly throwing away. Generally speaking, we don't pay too much attention to how much rubbish we generate, to the swift turnover of our material possessions or what happens to our waste. As you can imagine, the environmental impact of this cavalier approach is full on. It's estimated that in the UK we could feasibly recycle 50% of our household waste, but in actuality less than 9% gets recycled. Clearly it's time for a rethink.

An easy way to get your head round a green waste policy is to remember the trinity of eco-rubbish: reduce, reuse, recycle—in that order.

Maybe unglamorous, but all part of the green experience. A few small changes can go a long way.

Reducing rubbish from the outset saves lots of energy (both yours and the earth's) at the end. It's easy to do, and merely requires a more measured approach to shopping, a discerning eye to avoid over-packaged goods, and buying good quality long-lasting items where possible. Reusing products may at first seem a bit too thrifty and worthy, but what it loses in the instant gratification of new purchases it makes up for by decreasing mess and clutter and saving the pennies. Recycling is an obvious and accessible form of waste disposal. Almost all UK cities and towns now have a kerbside recycling service, and most councils are willing to make one-off collections. If you can't see any sign of a recycling policy in your locality, get in contact with your council. If they don't operate any systems, ask why, and look for a lobbying group (one's bound to exist) or find another scheme.

BLOT ON THE LANDSCAPE
—A BRIEF HISTORY OF RUBBISH

So just to recap: we are very talented at creating vast quantities of rubbish, but then fail to recycle 91% of it. So obviously the question is: what happens to all our waste? Thinking this through, and having a mental picture of the blot on the landscape our disposable lifestyles cause, is also a useful aid to remembering why we should be recycling!

Around 23 million tonnes (82% of the non-recycled quantity) of our waste ends up in landfill sites every year. These large holes provide a massive dumping ground for kinds of rubbish, but sadly that's not the end of the story. Huge amounts of materials like plastic and glass are not biodegradable, or at least not for hundreds of years. Those substances which do break down, such as organic waste, degrade to form leachate, which is a potent pollutant: alongside other chemicals and bacteria from rubbish, it can seep into the soil. Materials that degrade in landfill sites also produce methane—a so-called 'greenhouse gas', which contributes to global warming. These dumps are traditionally based far away from towns (and from expensive land), but this doesn't mean that urbanites should disregard them, as aside from the problems we have already looked at, the transportation of rubbish to the areas produces even more pollution.

Obviously, landfill sites are fraught with problems. Aside from the fact that we can't afford to turn over increasingly large amounts of land to house our debris, the health and pollution implications have caused the EC to seriously consider the place of landfill sites in the future. By 2016, EC laws dictate that the percentage of rubbish housed on

landfill sites must be decreased to 35%. This means that more and more councils are looking to incinerators to burn up our rubbish. But yes, you've guessed it—the effects of incinerating all those materials, including chemically-produced plastic, is believed to be extremely hazardous. Needless to say, residents near existing or proposed incinerators are very uneasy about the practice. Not only are there problems of potentially toxic fumes in their surrounding area but incinerators do not eliminate waste: 10% of the burned waste becomes ash which must be disposed of in landfill sites anyway, whilst a further 5% becomes what's known as 'fly ash' and must be disposed of as hazardous waste.

RECYCLED V RECYCLABLE

There's yet another logo to take on board here. Known as the 'mobius loop', this stylish little symbol features a circle of arrows. If the arrows are on a dark background then you know that the packaging has been recycled. If the arrows are on a light background then you know that the packaging is suitable for recycling. This is a helpful distinction if you bear in mind that just because something can be recycled in an ideal world (allowing it to boast the logo) doesn't mean that—in our very far from ideal world—it actually will be. In a nutshell, it is better to buy actual recycled products where possible so that you know the cycle has already been completed.

Plastic, as usual, is a more complicated scenario. Not all types of plastic can be recycled at the moment, and hybrid versions—even if the majority of the product is made of recyclable plastic—won't melt down properly, so can't be used. Strangely (although perhaps unsurprisingly, given our throw-away society), the idea of recycling plastic was only broached relatively recently. It seems to be something of a hot potato, where problems of inefficiency and creating even more pollution mean that there are still a lot of fundamental problems that need to be ironed out. But if we can recognize the plastics that can be recycled as opposed to those that can't, it gives us another opportunity to make informed shopping decisions. Not only will a plastic product feature the recycling logo, but it will also have a number in the centre of it which designates the type of plastic it's made from. Only three types of plastic can successfully be recycled at the moment:

- PET (polyethylene terephalate)—usually found in waterproof packaging.

- HDPE (high density polyethylene)—ubiquitous plastic found everywhere from washing up liquid bottles to plastic bags and toys.

- LDPE (low density polyethylene)—plastic bags, especially in clothes shops.

WATCHING YOUR WASTE

Some people are avid recyclers. For them, dealing with household rubbish is no problem, as they swiftly separate aluminium, glass and paper into their various bins. And then they complete the cycle, striving to buy recycled products. Others (the majority of us) have a more sporadic approach to recycling. Indeed, it seems to go through peaks and troughs of popularity: look at the late 1980s, where it suddenly became fashionable to seek out recycled cards and wrapping paper, and to get your cosmetic bottles refilled. However, if we are going to make a difference, we too are going to have to adopt a zero tolerance policy to rubbish, starting in the immediate environment of our homes.

The radical recyclers mentioned above might intimidate us with their rubbish-sorting prowess, but they can also provide some useful tips. One of the most immediate and simple techniques for implementing a successful and workable recycling system at home is to cut down on the volume of waste you're producing in the first place. This gives us another chance to use our consumer power. Product designers, manufacturers and marketing teams are adept at convincing us that we can't live without their products—after all, this is their mission in life. However, truly innovative, life-enhancing products are very few and far between, and most 'new' or 'better than ever' inventions are fairly average rehashes of something that was already there before. One way to get us to buy these new necessities is through clever packaging, making the product appear more attractive, but also by giving it other properties: convenient separate sachets, drip-free bottles, a plastic ball to bring the liquid closer to the wash, straight into the oven trays, a handy carrying case. All of these might have the effect of saving a couple of seconds in one way or another, but the packaging is resource- and energy-intensive, and often made up of substances that either take hundreds of years to biodegrade, or emit toxic (and some say carcinogenic) fumes when burned. Manufacturers and retailers can be prosecuted for over-packaging, although in practice this is something that happens very rarely. It does, however, give us another chance to exercise our purchasing power and demonstrate to manufacturers that far from being impressed by their increasingly ingenious ways of wasting more and more precious resources, we'd rather give them a miss completely.

BOX CLEVER

Remember that here, less is definitely more. Add the issue of packaging to your new eco-shopping list criteria. To take the industry out of shopping around, you should find that green and organic stores sell responsibly packaged goods as a matter of course (if not, then there's something seriously amiss). When you begin to consider the benefits of individually segregated doses of laundry fluid, it really doesn't seem to be such a life-saver. Stick to recycled or at least recyclable boxes, tins and jars where possible. Start on a small level by recycling plastic carrier bags in the supermarket. Or (as plastic bags don't exactly scream sartorial elegance) you might think about ditching them altogether and buying a couple of large and more attractive canvas shopping bags that you can use every time. As well as raising you up in the shopping/glamour stakes, they're much easier to carry.

CAN CAN

If you want full marks for recycling, make sure you save those drink cans. Aluminium, derived from bauxite, fetches the highest price of any recyclable packaging—recycling the cans uses only 10% of the energy used in manufacturing new ones (and you're reducing the need for more bauxite mining).

TOP TIPS FOR RECYCLING

• Remember the three Rs of green rubbish: reduce, reuse and recycle.

• Less is more. Cut down on the waste you bring into your home in the first place by adopting a zero tolerance policy on over-the-top packaging.

• Swap plastic carrier bags for a couple of all-purpose large canvas bags which you can take on every shopping trip.

• Harness the power of a compost heap or bin (see Chapter 3, Growing Without Pains), and recycle your kitchen waste.

• Use car boot sales and charity shops to keep the recycling wheel turning. If you are feeling very altruistic, then donate those unwanted clothes and toys to a charity shop; alternatively, if your commercial instincts won't be put to bed, sell them at a car boot sale. But remember that this doesn't work if you de-junk only to go out and purchase new, disposable stuff. You need to start scouring second-hand stores, charity shops and car boot sales yourself to complete the cycle. Fortunately vintage is a big style trend!

• Cut down on those annoying and environmentally pesky junk mail letters. You can prevent your daily deluge of uninteresting correspondence by removing your name from their databases. Contact the Mailing Preference Service (020 7766 4410).

• Instigate a new way of dealing with rubbish in your house or flat, and try and team up with some neighbours. Find out if a kerbside collection scheme operates in your area, as will be the case in most urban districts. You can do this by contacting your local authority, or try Wasteline on 0870 243 0136 for further information. If your council hasn't made any provisions for collecting rubbish for recycling, hassle them until they do.

• Once you've got your weekly collection sorted, get used to collecting and sorting your rubbish so that all recyclable materials are in the right place to enable the scheme to work more efficiently.

- Use recycling banks. These can be found in many supermarket car parks and shopping centres; they collect a variety of materials, from the standard glass and newspapers, through to textiles. Make sure that the recycling banks you use are regularly emptied and are not just an eco-show that doesn't do very much.

OFFICE POLITICS

Once you've got a successful, stress-free recycling system going at home, you'll probably find it hard to leave it there. Don't be surprised if you feel a sudden and overwhelming desire to start implementing similar changes in the office. Despite the much-lauded paperless office, system errors and a lack of confidence in computers mean that most of us are psychologically unable to abandon our habit of using vast quantities of paper as back-up. Remember that small is beautiful, and even if you begin by recycling paper in your plain paper fax machine (remember to put it in the right way), that's a very positive start. Cut up old paper for notes rather than starting a new notebook, and wherever possible try and bring in some recycled stationery. Some companies now sell cartridges which have been remanufactured or are refillable; or you can recycle used cartridges and donate them to charity at the same time.

Stationery made from old circuit boards.

At the very least, make sure your company has a recycling scheme in place so that all that paper is being collected.

THE GREAT OUTDOORS

You may live in the thick of things, right at the hub, at the epicentre of a vibrant town or city, but whether for reasons of work or leisure you will no doubt need to travel around. This could be a matter of going to the other side of your urbanscape to visit friends, getting to your office, or maybe visiting a different town. Whatever the reason, we need to be more mobile now than ever before. Travel is a question of personal freedom as much as necessity, and we demand the right to move freely about our immediate environment, across the country and even around the globe. However, while we may have become increasingly mobile we have of course paid a heavy price by polluting our environment.

WALK THIS WAY

Those boots were made for walking. Bizarrely, even though we urbanites hate sitting in traffic jams, we seem to feel compelled to jump in our cars to make the shortest of journeys at the busiest of times. It can be fantastically liberating to rediscover the power of walking. For short journeys it's the most time-efficient travel method, as well as boosting the heart rate. Personal safety is now a big issue everywhere, and these concerns have to be squared with environmental factors. Start walking and campaigning for pedestrian safety, including crossings, pavements and street lighting. To cut down on needless car journeys we need to reclaim the pavements for pedestrians.

CAR DO'S AND DON'TS

• If you live near decent transport links, you may feel brave enough to dispense with driving a car altogether—after all, they're not only hugely damaging to the environment but vastly expensive by the time you've paid for city insurance, tax and maintenance.

• If you can't give up your car, make sure it is the most eco-friendly model you can get your hands on. Unless you are a part-time farmer who does serious time in the sticks, you shouldn't really need a mammoth 4-wheel drive number. These increase fuel consumption by around 5%, but it is surprising how many urbanites feel the need to drive them around congested towns and cities and park them all over the pavements.

• Suburbanites should refrain from driving into the city to do their shopping. Park and Ride sounds like a fairly jaded concept after many years, but these schemes are still bussing people into many towns, and they work. A few pence will take you from your car straight into the shopping area and back again, and save you the hassle and heartache of finding that elusive parking space in the city centre.

- Keep your car up to scratch. A regularly serviced car in proper working order will be less polluting.

- It's the small things that count—regular tune-ups and regular oil changes help to minimize a car's effect on the environment.

- Bald tyres are dangerous (and illegal) and definitely not fuel-efficient. Make sure tyres are in good health, balanced and aligned, so they'll be as fuel-efficient as they can be.

- Boy racers, petrol heads, speed demons and Top Gear fans should find a new hobby rather than discussing respective engine sizes. No doubt the thrill of zooming along the open road in a high performance or souped-up mobile can be exhilarating. But the reality is that the volume of traffic on UK roads is such that we rarely get to experience the open road at all. Sitting in traffic jams whilst your high performance car contributes some serious emissions to the rest of the planet is distinctly unfriendly behaviour.

DITCHING THE CAR

Experiencing serious congestion on a daily basis, driving round searching for elusive parking spaces that don't require some sort of permit, and forking out high insurance and road tax payments, have of course been enough to put a number of people off the idea of owning a car altogether. Some councils are planning even more draconian measures to reduce the volume of traffic in our towns and cities (look at the plan to charge Londoners £5 to drive into the city centre), and such is the ferocity of such campaigns that you can imagine a day in the not-too-distant future when it just won't be feasible for many urbanites to have a car at all.

On the face of it these measures may seem unjust, curtailing our rights and personal freedom. However, there can be no denying that traffic is choking our cities and towns and it would be in all our best interests to keep as much space as possible pedestrianized. Ditching our cars would enhance our air quality, allow us to avoid congestion, eliminate hundreds of accidents and save us personally a lot of money. Put like this, the green option sounds quite attractive, until you remember the gripe that we all share—public transport. It is an understatement to complain that public transport falls far below both our expectations and needs. In fact in some areas it has become so bad that it actually threatens our safety; and it certainly compromises our lifestyles, as we are unable, at the most basic level, to get to the office and back again on time. It's a catch-22 situation. The system won't get any better until we put in enough money, time and support, and we're understandably reluctant to do this as it's so bad. Rather than digging our heels in, we urbanites need to get out of our cars and start lobbying for better transport.

POOL YOUR RESOURCES

Let's face it: in this day and age, the need to use a car often arises. Although as a society we need to cut our car use dramatically (and you may be able to dispense with your car altogether, saving yourself a lot of money in the process), it is almost certain you'll need to travel in a car from time to time. One solution is to join an existing car pool, or set up your own. Not only does this cut down on individual cost and effort, but it also makes sense environmentally—after all, why drive five cars when you can take one? Try <www.car-pool.co.uk> to find out if there is an existing car pool you can get involved with. Otherwise, you could begin by sounding out friends, neighbours, family or colleagues to see if you can come up with your own.

GET ON YOUR BIKE

The eco-friendly way of maintaining your personal mobility, scooting through city traffic and keeping very fit, is of course to get on your bike. There can be no denying that cyclists are very vulnerable, especially in urban traffic where a great many drivers seem to disregard them altogether. Therefore it's important to make sure you know what you're doing as you need to be one step ahead of the game.

If you haven't ridden for a while (e.g. circa 1970), remember that although allegedly you never forget how to ride a bike, your skills might need honing slightly. Sign up for a cycling proficiency course, and learn the proper rules of the road, which will help you avoid trouble in the future. You may also want to update the rickety old cycle from the shed in favour of a more contemporary model (see below) which will make it easier to manoeuvre and to ride in general—and will save you from any sticky situations such as failing brakes or vital components flying off as you're free-wheeling down a hill. Use cycling lanes and specially designated routes where possible, and when you've really got into cycling mode you might become enthused enough to lobby your local council to give cyclists even better facilities on the roads.

TOP TIPS FOR BUYING A NEW BIKE

If you've decided that two wheels are the way forward, you can consider shelling out for a decent piece of equipment that will save you puffing up hills in the wrong gear.

• Heading down to your local bike shop seems like the obvious solution. Experts suggest that you try to suss out the shop assistants first and make sure that they are knowledgeable cycling enthusiasts rather than just staff on commission. Also check out deals that offer after-sale care, such as a free service after you have had the bike for a number of weeks.

• Don't over-bike. When faced with a new, exciting hobby, the temptation is always there to run out and buy the meanest, leanest, hill climbing machine you can get your hands on. However groovy that pink mountain bike might first appear, it may not be the most practical device for whizzing round the city. Get clued up on what's available so that you can find something that will serve your purposes well.

A 21st century bicycle salesman.

BIKE MANIA

Sadly, bike mania can cause bike maniacs. Nicknamed Lycra louts, there are a number of road and pavement hogs who cause road chaos by dangerous cycling. Whilst cyclists have a very real grudge against inconsiderate and plain aggressive motorists, bike maniacs give cycling a bad name and weaken the cause. It's important to remember that you can be prosecuted for dangerous riding, not just driving, so you should make sure you're knowledgeable about the rules of the road. Obviously, if you understand what's going on at major junctions you're going to be much safer.

BIKE POOL

Brilliant but obvious, speedy but clean—the bike pool is seen as the way forward for a number of councils. London's Camden Council is just one of the organizations which has scrapped expensive, polluting car pools in favour of a collection of bikes which can be booked out by members of staff who have appointments all over the borough.

REAL PEDAL POWER

Bicycles are an eco-friendly, fitness-enhancing solution for many urban-ites—but not all of them. Health problems and age considerations means that we can't all be expected to reach our physical peaks (some of us may well be past them!) in the saddle. A 'Powabyke' might well be your answer. It's an electric solution, so obviously there are some environmental issues, but it is distinctly the lesser of many evils. A battery can be charged in a socket slotted on to the bike, which has a normal frame. The bike (or trike) rides normally, but you can decide when you need an extra boost by turning the handle and getting an electric kick from the battery.

• The Electric Bike Centre, Pleiades, 3 West Hill, London SW18 1RB. Tel: 020 8870 2138.

SMART CITY DRIVING

Somewhere between eco-ideologist and the wanton petrol guzzler sits the Smart Car enthusiast. Smart Cars are the dinky little numbers that have added a bit of 'small is beautiful chic' to city roads in the last couple of years. At 2.5 metres long, they are at least one metre shorter than any other car, and can fit in the weeniest of parking spaces— which saves on circling that block fifteen times like a parking vulture. Not surprisingly, the smallest car is also the most fuel-efficient, radically cutting down on fuel emissions. There are some drawbacks: it's only a two-seater, and until recently has been difficult to get hold of right hand drive models. There is also an electric cut-off, so you can't accelerate above 85 mph—but why would you need to? If you can't face being without your motor but are willing to scale down, find out more about the Smart range. Tel: 0800 037 9966 or <www.thesmart.co.uk>.

diary: carless in london

It's a nasty admission, but I have rarely been without a car in the last eight years. Even worse is the fact that due to financial restrictions my cars have tended to be decrepit, fuel-guzzling, inefficient monstrosities. Finally, perhaps most terrible of all is the fact that I live in London next to all manner of public transport options.

But if I want to give myself a break and find some mitigating circumstances, all I need to do is think about some of my experiences on the tube and rail network. As I usually travel to work by overground train, I am well versed in the excuses behind the almost daily delays which occur on my journeys. Many days there is no excuse at all—just no train, and without any information we have to stand in the rain for half an hour.

However, the issue has been forced now because our car has officially turned into a piece of rubbish. It no longer starts, every surface has rusted and I don't really want to be seen in it anyway—I have noticed a number of friends turn down lifts recently. Consequently we have taken the very brave step of doing without a car!

Our experiment officially begins when we have to pay somebody to come and remove the beast. They then strip the car of whatever useful parts they can find and shred the rest of it, after removing the environmentally damaging stuff. Sadly, because of the age and type of the car, and because breakers yards don't have enough of a recycling capacity, some of the car will no doubt end up in a landfill. I console myself that at least we won't be driving around in it any more.

Ben is lucky enough to work from home—which is perhaps the perfect eco-friendly solution! But though I usually take the train to work during the week, I decide to invest in a weekly travel pass to cover my extra-curricular weekend travel. Top tip: on a Monday morning get to the station early so you actually have time to get through all the administration, or better still do it on a Sunday night! I will next time.

After a few days of train delays, bus overcrowding and general inconvenience I have decided a) to always carry an A-Z map; b) to get clued up on bus timetables; and c) to try cycling. Having spent what must amount to several weeks in traffic jams, I was always faintly envious of those cyclists

diary

whizzing past, although this diminished in the wind and rain. Fearing that our fitness levels might not be up to scratch at first, Ben and I have decided to try out some e-power—that's electric bikes, in case you were wondering.

We head down to Putney to the Electric Bike centre to test out some elec- 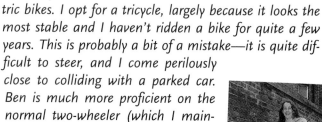 tric bikes. I opt for a tricycle, largely because it looks the most stable and I haven't ridden a bike for quite a few years. This is probably a bit of a mistake—it is quite difficult to steer, and I come perilously close to colliding with a parked car. Ben is much more proficient on the normal two-wheeler (which I maintain is much easier). For a very simple concept, it's impressively effective. Built exactly like a normal bike with the exception of a rather large battery, you can basically turn on the  power when you need it. The only drawback I could find was that it does sound like a milk float!

Six weeks later . . .

I have to concede that I've actually quite enjoyed not having a car. Having two wheels instead of four does take quite a load of the mind: insurance, tax, services, breakdown, parking etc. The downside is of course travel delays on public transport, and at the risk of coming across as 'disgusted of Tunbridge Wells', I have even been moved to send emails to the customer services departments of train companies!

Now that the opportunity to jump in a car to go small distances has, well, been physically removed, my fitness has soared just by walking—so much so that we have finally invested in some push-bikes. Although I still feel too nervous to venture on to main roads without cycle lanes, I have found it liberating to see a city I know so well without being confined to a car, bus or train. Whether this sense of freedom will continue in the sleet and snow remains to be seen.

the greenhouse effect—bristol

The Federation of City Farms and Community Gardens has been supporting and advising community farm and garden initiatives across the UK for the past 20 years. This is the organization with the know-how, supplying training, advice and support for the four city farms in the Federation's hometown of Bristol, fourteen in London, and at least one in almost all cities and major towns in the UK.

The GreenHouse in Bristol is the Federation's permanent base. But this is no model city farm; unlike most others, there are not even any animals here. This is a deliberate departure to emphasize the fact that every city farm is unique and specific to its own urban environment. So whilst The GreenHouse provides the headquarters for the federation, it's not a blueprint for farms elsewhere.

Instead, The GreenHouse provides a permanent office space, a resource centre with

a library, and a training and meeting place. The facilities are also hired out to a large number of other organizations, which generates income and exposes even more people to the concept behind City Farms. As you would expect, The GreenHouse has impeccable eco-credentials, including a grass roof, an environmentally friendly structure made from sustainable, European wood, and a design which utilizes every last shaft of natural daylight.

Although the idea of city farms and gardens may seem like a simple one, the projects in each area can actually be quite complex, running far deeper than just addressing environmental concerns. Education is a key point of the centres, especially as volunteers could well be growing food and plants for the first time. The schemes are unusual in that   they are genuinely inclusive, reflecting a whole cross section of urban life and giving a whole range of people access to green spaces.

One of the main points behind city farm and garden projects is to ensure that urbanites have access to real green spaces. As research has proved, limited access to the natural environment can be a major contributor to stress, a problem exacerbated by inner city living, where access is restricted to start with. The Federation takes account of the fact that true access means an environment that caters for local needs, and is not just cosmetically green and pretty. So whilst many schemes will have pockets of space such as wildlife sanctuaries which are regularly out of bounds, there will also be well designed, well planted areas with play or growing areas where everyone can make use of the space.

Details from: The GreenHouse, Hereford St, Bristol BS3 4NA. Tel: 0117 923 1800. <www.farmgarden.org.uk>.

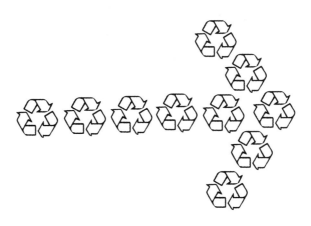

Chapter 8

the final
countdown

Congratulations, urban junglist! You've made it to the end of the green experience! Hopefully you're feeling at least light green, and possibly you've gone the whole hog by installing a compost toilet and wind turbine in your garden. Alternatively, you may not have done anything yet, in which case order that recycling box today at the very least. But whatever you do, sustainability counts here as well. Small, considered gestures that you can live with will underpin your green lifestyle and ensure it for the future.

diary: six months and counting

Sometimes looking back can fill you with a certain sense of pride and a smug satisfaction. This is because you can kind of filter out all the bad bits (box schemes full of aubergines, slugs attacking your tomatoes, cycling on a dark winter morning when the weather's doing a very good impression of a monsoon). But as this is quite a satisfying feeling, I've decided to go with the rose-tinted specs and focus on the positive experiences. . . .

Wild food: we have made great strides forward in terms of changing our diet to something that is around 75% organic. Finding a good local box scheme made all the difference to us. They research all their suppliers thoroughly and will try and get UK produce wherever possible. As they go to the storehouses themselves, our box schemers know individual customer requirements, and if something on your list isn't available they'll replace it with a comparable item. This avoids the disappointment when your fruit and veg box arrives full of mouldy aubergines, etc. There's still a bit of work to be done, as bad habits occasionally sneak back, but we have finally severed that

How green are you feeling? Whether you're still in the light green zone, or have gone the whole hog and become the ultimate urban junglist, let's hope you've laid some strong green foundations.

---- diary ----

cord to the supermarket in favour of green stores and whenever possible fresh food markets. Of course, we are lucky to be close to three or four outstanding markets where the variety and quality of fresh, UK-sourced produce continues to astound me. I would find it almost impossible to return to our former shopping and eating habits, and have no desire to, despite the fact that we are now spending more on our weekly shopping. But because we are much more organized about the whole process of shopping, cooking, storing and freezing our food, the cost goes down considerably because we're no longer wasting so much.

I found the process of growing some vegetables and herbs much more exciting than anyone else I know! My over-enthusiasm was really down to the fact that I assumed I would be horticulturally challenged—I had never done it before, and thought there was some great mystery to growing things. Of course experience counts for a lot, and the more you know the more easily and successfully you will be able to grow, but even for first-timers it's possible to grow a really useful batch of herbs in containers with the minimum of fuss. Whilst I'm certainly not ready for the intensive labour required on an allotment, I think container gardening is something I will stick with as you really can't beat the convenience of snipping off some herbs from the window box and throwing them in a sauce.

One of the more abstract effects on our lives of this whole project is to sort of liberate us from our immediate surroundings. Once you start focusing on green spaces in the urban environment, it stands to reason that you will check them out and start to make increasing use of whatever natural outdoor spaces there are. You also start to get to know your city or town much better than you did before. This is certainly what has happened to us. We've acquired new knowledge about cycle routes, walking routes (<www.ramblers.org.uk> can advise), outdoor tennis courts or just park spaces to run in. Making urban landscapes accessible is an important part of greening your life. It's also supposed to make you less anxious and stressed (too early for me to comment on this, I'm afraid), but there is definitely something to be said for reclaiming a bit of the great outdoors. Experts also claim that the fitness benefits are greater from working out outside on a natural terrain rather than on a treadmill in the gym (contact <www.greengym.org.uk> to find out about outdoor fitness initiatives combined with conservation projects).

Whilst the restricted dimensions of our living quarters haven't altered, at least we have managed to get rid of a lot of our junk. Another home innovation has been our seagrass flooring throughout the flat, replacing our horrid old carpet—I used to start off the day by sneezing loudly in quick succession for about 30 minutes followed up by frantic eye-rubbing, as my allergies kicked

diary

in. These do seem to have abated, but as I haven't carried out experiments in laboratory conditions I really can't say whether my new allergy-free existence is due to natural floorcovering, green cleaners or natural bedding, or maybe a combination of everything—but it's definitely a big plus!

I was quite distraught recently when I found out that my favourite organic night spot had closed. Centrally located, with a very good, well designed restaurant upstairs and a bar and club area downstairs, it managed to be completely organic without appearing disconcertingly worthy. However, every cloud has a silver lining as they say, and closer investigation reveals that it has closed as the company are moving to a bigger premises and opening two more bars early next year!

Green shopping may have curbed my impulsive tendencies—never again will I be able to randomly purchase without paying heed to ethical or environmental concerns! Fortunately, thanks to a lovely range of all manner of green products from mail order, specialist stores and the internet, I can still indulge in some retail therapy when the need arises.

OK, so we're still a long way from installing solar panels on the roof but we have made some substantial changes in a relatively short time with the minimum of expense and fuss, which were key points for us. The results are not breathtaking, but they are significant. They have also put us in contact with a whole host of green organizations, resources and information bodies which will help when it comes to future projects. Urban life is fraught with stresses, problems and compromises, as we all know. A greener approach won't solve all these problems, but it will bring a chemical-free calmness and considered approach to our frazzled lives. We've found the benefits far outweigh the negatives, and I'd urge anyone to have a go. Get greening!

GLOSSARY OF TERMS
IN THE URBAN JUNGLE

Blue Peter Syndrome
Ability to make draught excluders and other examples of practical creativity gleaned from years of watching the popular children's TV programme.

Clever Cosmetics
Eco, chemical-free alternatives to the myriad of conventional lotions and potions we like to buy.

Clutter Buster
A strategy for ridding your house or flat of all that rubbish you have accumulated. Tackling the issue head-on by sorting out unwanted clothes, textiles, books and toys and selling them off at a car boot sale or donating them to charity shops.

De-junk
As above.

DIY Deluge
The huge variety of interior design TV programmes, books and magazines which all feed the craze for DIY.

Eco-Chic
Relatively new concept that green, eco-friendly design can transcend that hippy-dippy stereotype of old to embrace contemporary design and style.

Eco-Tip
Abstract ability to imagine the waste a product will create before purchasing, and assessing recyclability etc.

E-power
Electric power required when conventional car has been ditched but fitness levels dictate that some assistance is needed.

Funky Farmer
Has abandoned straw chewing and 19th century tweed jacket in favour of radical new image. Will often supplement meagre earnings of farming by yoga teaching or IT-related business.

Green Clean
Way of keeping everything spick and span in the home without pouring nasty chemicals and toxic concoctions on your vital surfaces.

Greenscene
The burgeoning, increasingly dynamic network of bars, restaurants, pubs and juice bars catering for the green and organic enthusiast. Provides an eco-hangout that doesn't involve making compost or growing root vegetables.

Guerrilla Gardening
Activity for people who don't wait to be asked. They are so keen to plant in the urban environment and reclaim inner city space that they may plant without permission.

Home Truths
The shocking reality of the chemicals pervading our personal sanctuaries in the carpets to the curtains.

Lycra Louts
Name attributed to aggressive cyclists who ride at high speeds on pavements and other areas they shouldn't be on, and generally flout the rules of the road.

Mean Streets
Dramatic description of the urban outdoors and the reason we like to shut it all out when we get home.

Maxi Makeover
Big changes that will turn any home into an eco-sanctuary of the highest order.

Mini Makeover
Smaller changes to a light green home for immediate eco-effects.

Pedal Power
Novel approach for motorists that involves using their own bodies to get mobile and uses two wheels rather than an emission-belching four.

Smart Cars
Chic mini-beast of a car designed to fit in the slightest of spaces, cut congestion by its very smallness and reduce emissions.

Spatially Challenged
Personal environment of the majority of urbanites, who have sensibly decided to live in highly expensive places, which eats into their wages as land is at a premium.

Toxic Overload
Undesirable condition which we approach as we continue to imbibe and ingest a whole concoction of weird substances.

Tree-Hugger
Traditional image of an environmentally concerned person with comic potential. May also wear a kaftan and or tie-dye.

The Three Rs
Holy trinity of waste-watching: reduce, reuse and recycle. Forget them at your peril!

Urban Jungle
The vast sprawling metropolis, suburban sidestreets or ordered towns where we choose to hang out. Characterized by their lack of pastoral vistas.

Urbanite
Person who resides in any of the above stress-inducing, expensive pollution zones.

Wild Food
Produce that defies the convention of being created from a concoction of chemicals that invest it with unreasonable qualities of longevity. Warning: this food may have a natural taste derived from the ground, tree or animal of origin.

Zero Tolerance
No-nonsense policy to ensure that green intentions don't fall by the wayside.

MINI DIRECTORY

The following chapter-by-chapter guide will give you links and stockist information for most of the projects mentioned, additional contact information and some extra reading in case you have been inspired to take further action!

Chapter 1: Absolute Beginners

Biodynamic Agricultural Association (BDAA), Painswick Inn Project, Stroud, Glos GL5 1QG. Tel: 01453 759 501. <www.anth.org.uk/biodynamic>.

Green Guide Publishing, 271 Upper Street, London N1 2UQ. Tel: 020 7354 2709. <www.thegreenguideonline.com>. Comprehensive shopping directory for London, the South-west, North-west, North-east, Midlands, South-east, East Anglia, Wales and Scotland.

Pure, a bi-monthly consumer magazine devoted to organic food, natural health and eco-living, available from news-stands or call Green Guide Publishing (see above).

The Ecologist, <www.theecologist.org> or contact subscriptions 01795 414 963. The world's longest running environmental magazine. Monthly issues available from news stands, bookshops and selected retailers.

Friends of the Earth, 26–28 Underwood Street, London N1 7JQ. Tel: 020 7490 1555. <info@foe.co.uk> <www.foe.co.uk>.

Greenpeace, Canonbury Villas, London N1 2PN. Tel: 020 7865 8100. <www.greenpeace.org.uk>.

The Organic Directory, <www.theorganicdirectory.co.uk>. A county-by-county guide to organic retailers, producers, restaurants, etc. Published by Green Books with the Soil Association.

Resurgence, Rocksea Farmhouse, St. Mabyn, Cornwall, PL30 3BR. Tel: 01208 841824. <subs@resurge@virgin.net> <www.resurgence.org>. A great fount of environmental thinking, with an artistic and spiritual bent—check it out.

Soil Association, Bristol House, 40–56 Victoria Street, Bristol BS1 6BY. Tel: 0117 929 0661 Fax: 0117 925 2504. <info@soilassociation.org> <www.soilassociation.org>.

Willing Workers on Organic Farms (WWOOF), PO Box 2675, Lewes, East Sussex BN7 1RB. <www.pwnninw.oef.uk/wwoof.htm>.

Chapter 2: Go Wild With Food

Big Barn Ltd, College Farm, Great Barford, Bedford MK44 3JJ. Tel: 01234 872 005. <www.bigbarn.co.uk>. Virtual farmers' market.

Helen Browning/Eastbrook Organic Meat, Eastbrook Farm, Bishopstone, Swindon SN6 8PW. Tel: 01793 790 460 Fax: 01793 791 239. <www.helen-browningorganics.co.uk>. Large variety of organic meat.

The Campaign For Real Food, c/o Positive PR, 3 The Castle House, Long Street, Sherborne, Dorset DT9 3BU. Tel: 01935 389 497.

Capricorn Organics, Tel: 020 8306 3786. <www.capricornorganics.co.uk>. Box Scheme established in 1995. Provides UK grown organic produce wherever possible. Delivers to South and South East London.

The Food Commission, 94 White Lion Street, London N1 9PF. Tel: 020 7837 2250. <foodcomm@compuserve.com> <www.foodcomm.org.uk>. Campaigns for safer and healthier food in the UK.

Fresh & Wild stores are in Camden, Old Street, Lavender Hill, Notting Hill, Soho and Stoke Newington. Tel: 0800 9175 175. <www.freshandwild.com>.

Graig Farm Organics, Dolau, Llandrindod Wells, Powys. Tel: 01597 851 655. <www.graigfarm.co.uk>. Sells organic produce by mail order.

Grassroots, 20 Woodlands Road, Glasgow. Tel: 0141 353 3278. Award-winning organic store.

Meanwood Valley Urban Farm, Sugarwell Road, Meanwood, Leeds LS7 2QG. Tel: 0113 262 9759.

National Association of Farmers' Markets, South Vaults, Green Park Station, Green Park Road, Bath BA1 1JB. <www.farmersmarkets.net>. Tel: 01225 787 914.

Neal's Yard Dairy, 6 Park St, Borough Market, London SE1 and 19 Shorts Gardens, London, WC2H 9UP. Tel: 020 7645 3564. <www.nealsyarddairy.co.uk>. Mail order: 020 7645 3555 <mailorder@nealsyarddairy.co.uk>.

The Organic Bustop, 114 Landor Road, Clapham, London SW9. Tel: 020 7274 8891. Specialist lifestyle retailer; also runs a box scheme.

Organics Direct, <www.organicsdirect.co.uk>. Winner of the 1999 Soil Association Box Scheme of the Year award. Also supplies a full range of green groceries.

The Organic Food Federation, 31 Turbine Way, EcoTech Business Park, Swaffham, Norfolk PE37 7XD. Tel: 01760 720 444. <www.orgfoodfed.org>.

The Organic Trust Ltd, Vernon House, 2 Vernon Avenue, Clontarf, Dublin 3. Tel: (+353) 01 853 0271.

Penrhos Court, Kington, Herefordshire HR5 3LH. Tel: 01544 230720. <daphne@penrhos.co.uk> <www.penrhos.co.uk>. An organic centre with hotel, restaurant and school, which runs food and health courses and eco-organic events.

Pesticide Residues Committee, <www.pesticides.gov.uk>. Government pesticide surveillance.

Planet Organic, 42 Westbourne Grove, London W2. Tel: 020 7727 2227. and 22 Torrington Place, London WC1. Tel: 020 7436 1929. Mail order: 020 7221 1345.

Simply Organic Food Company, Unit A62-64, New Covent Garden Market, London SW8 5EE. Tel 0845 1000 444. <info@simplyorganic.net> <www.simplyorganic.net>. The UK's largest home delivery organic supermarket.

The Village Bakery, Melmerby, Penrith CA10 1HE. Tel: 01768 881515. <admin@village-bakery.com> <www.village-bakery.com>. Specialist bakers or organic bread and cakes.

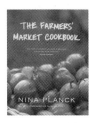

READING:
The Farmers' Market Cookbook by Nina Planck (Hodder & Stoughton)

Chapter 3: Growing Without Pains

Federation of City Farms and Community Gardens, The GreenHouse, Hereford Street, Bedminster, Bristol BS3 4NA. Tel: 0117 923 1800. <www.farmgarden.org.uk>.

Henry Doubleday Research Association (HDRA), Ryton Organic Gardens, Ryton-on-Dunsmore, Coventry CV8 3LG. Tel: 02476 303517. <www.hdra.org.uk>.

Also at: Yalding Organic Gardens, Benover Lane, Yalding, Maidstone, Kent ME18 6EX. Tel: 01622 814650.
and Audley End Organic Kitchen Garden, Saffron Walden, Essex CB11 4JF. Tel: 01799 520444.

National Society of Allotment and Leisure Gardeners (NSALG), Odell House, Hunters Road, Corby, Northants NN17 5JE. Tel: 01536 266 567. <www.nsalg.co.uk>.

The Organic Gardening Catalogue, Riverdene Business Park, Moseley Road, Hersham, Surrey KT12 4RG. Tel: 01932 253 666. <www.organicCatalog.com>.

READING:
Seeds: the ultimate guide to growing successfully from seed by Jekka McVicar (Kyle Cathie Ltd).

COMPOSTING:

Blackwall Products, 10 Glover Way, Parkside, Leeds LS11 5JP
Tel: 0113 276 1646.

Community Composting Network, 76 Alexandra Road, Sheffield S2 3EE.
Tel: 0114 258 0483. < ccn@gn.apc.org>.

Green Cone Ltd, Innovation House, Daleside Road, Nottingham NG2
4DH. Tel: 0115 911 4372. Sell food digesters, which take everything a
compost bin can't, and breaks it down.

Original Organics Ltd, Unit 9, Langlands Business Park, Uffculme,
Cullompton EX15 3DA. Tel: 01884 841 515. Specialize in bins and
wormeries.

Straight Recycling Systems, 31 Eastgate, Leeds LS 2 7LY. Tel: 0113 245
2244. <www.straight.co.uk>. Suppliers of compost bins and other
products.

READING:
Backyard Composting by John Roulac (Green Books)

Chapter 4: Living La Vida Verde

Auro Organic Paint Supplies, Unit 2, Pamphillions Farm, Debden, Saffron
Walden, Essex CB11 3JT. Tel: 01799 543 077. <www.auroorganic.co.uk>.

Centre for Alternative Technology, Machynlleth, Powys SY20 9AZ.
Tel: 01654 702400. <www.cat.org.uk>. Great visitor centre and big mail
order catalogue.

Ecological Building Centre, 16 Great Guildford Street, London SE1.
0207 450 2211. <www.ecoconstruct.com>.

Ecological Design Association, Slad Road, Stroud, Gloucestershire
GL5 1QW. Tel: 01453 765 575. Information and resource body.

The Energy Saving Trust & Solar Trade Association, 21 Dartmouth St, London SW1H 9BP. Tel: 020 7222 0101. <www.est.org.uk>.

The Environment Trust, Tel: 020 7377 0481.

The Green Building Store, 11 Huddersfield Road, Meltham, Holmfirth, West Yorkshire HD9 4NJ. Tel: 01484 854 898 Fax: 01484 854 899. <sales@greenbuildingstore.co.uk> <www.greenbuildingstore.co.uk>. Natural paint collection, timber finishes, varnish, primer and other green building and decorating supplies.

Juice Power, Tel: 0800 316 2610. <www.npower.com/juice>. Greenpeace has joined up with Npower to form a new green energy supply.

National Energy Foundation, The Energy Centre, Davy Ave, Knowlhill Road, Milton Keynes MK5 8NG. Tel: 01908 665 555. <www.greenenergy.org.uk> <www.solartradeassociation.org.uk>.

Salvo, <www.salvo.co.uk>. Salvage—guaranteed to find something for every room in the house.

Textiles from Nature, 84 Stoke Newington Church St, London N16 0AP. Tel: 020 72410990. <www.textilesfromnature.com>.

Texture, Tel: 020 7241 0990. <www.textilesfromnature.com>. Chemical-free fabrics.

Weiming Furniture, contemporary bamboo furniture. Tel: 01795 472262. <www.weimingfurniture.com>.

Women's Environmental Network, 87 Worship Street, London EC2A 2BE. Tel: 020 7481 9004. <wenuk@gn.apc.org> <www.gn.apc.org.wen>. Campaigns on food issues, waste, health and the environment, sanitary protection and nappies.

Chapter 5: Eco-Chic comes to Town

Ecology Building Society, 18 Station Road, Cross Hills, Keighley, West Yorks BD20 7EH. Tel: 0845 674 55566. <info@ecology.co.uk>. Provides green mortgages, including encouraging organic food production.

EcoZone, Birchwood House, Croydon, Surrey CR0 5AD. Tel: 0870 600 6969 Fax: 020 8777 3393. <www.ecozone.co.uk>. Sells all manner of green products, from clothes and cosmetics to wine and green gardening books. Order via phone, fax or website.

Ethical Consumer Research Association, Unit 21, 41 Old Birley Street, Manchester M15 5RF. Tel: 0161 226 2929. <www.ethicalconsumer.org>

The Fair Trade Foundation, Suite 204, 16 Baldwin's Gardens, London EC1N 7RJ. Tel: 020 7405 5942. <www.fairtrade.org.uk>.

The Green People Company, Brighton Road, Handcross, West Sussex RH17 6BZ. Tel: 01444 401 444. <www.greenpeople.co.uk>.

Greenfibres, 99 High Street, Totnes, Devon TQ9 5PF. Tel: 01803 868001. <www.greenfibres.com>. Clothes and other products from natural materials including hemp.

Dr Hauschka, Unit 19–20, Stockwood Business Park, Stockwood, Nr. Redditch B96 6FX. Tel: 01386 792 622. <www.drhauschka.co.uk>.

Jurlique, Willowtree Marina, West Quay Drive, Yeading, Middlesex UB4 9TB. Tel: 020 8841 6644. <www.jurlique.com.au>.

Kersaint Cobb, Gorsey Lane, Coleshill, Birmingham B46 1JU. Tel: 01675 430 222. Brochure hotline: 0800 028 5371.

Mulberry Bush Ltd, Newbridge Lodge, Billinghurst Road, Horsham RH12 3LN. Tel: 01403 754400. <www.mulberry-bush.com>.

Myriad, The Buckingham Building, 43 Southampton Road, Ringwood, BH24 1HE. Tel: 01725 517 085. <www.myriadonline.co.uk>. Natural toys.

Napiers Direct, 3 Queen Charlotte Lane, Edinburgh EH6 6AY. Tel: 0131 553 3500. <www.napiers.net>. Organic skin care and body care range.

Natural Collection, Eco House, Monmouth Place, Bath BA1 2DQ. Mail order. Tel: 0870 331 3333, Fax: 01225 469673. <www.naturalcollection.com>. The trading partner for Friends of the Earth and Greenpeace, featuring hundreds of green products and gifts.

Neal's Yard Remedies, 15 Neal's Yard, Covent Garden, WC2H 9DP. Also other shops in London and most major cities. Mail Order: 29 John Dalton Street, Manchester, M2 6DS. Tel: 0161 831 7875. Customer services: 020 7627 1949. <cservices@nealsyardremedies.com> <www.nealsyardremedies.com>.

Think Natural, Tel: 0845 601 1223. <www.ThinkNatural.com>. Comprehensive mail order service for wellbeing, outdoor, travel and home products.

Triodos Bank, 11 The Promenade, Clifton, Bristol BS8 3NN. Tel: 0800 3282181. <www.triodos.co.uk>. Ethical bank.

Weleda, Heanor Road, Ilkeston, Derbyshire DE7 8DR. Tel: 0115 944 8200. <www.weleda.co.uk>. Products available nationwide.

READING:
Eco-Renovation by Edward Harland (Green Books)

Chapter 6: Green Scene

The Freedom Brewing Company, 41 Earlham Street, Covent Garden, London WC2H 1LD. Tel: 020 7240 0606.
and at 14–16 Ganton Street, Carnaby St, London W1. Tel: 020 7287 5267.

The Crown, 223 Grove Road, London E3 Tel: 020 8981 9991. The first totally organic gastro-pub in Britain.

The Duke of Cambridge, 30 St Peter's Street, London N1. Tel: 020 7359 3066.

The HDRA Organic Wine Club, 261 Upper Town Street, Leeds LS13 3JT Tel: 0113 257 7545.

ORG, 79 Great George Street, Leeds LS1 3BR. Tel: 0113 234 700. <www.org-organics.org.uk>

Pitfield Organic Brewery, The Beer Shop, 14 Pitfield St, London N1 6EY. Tel: 020 7739 3701.

Vinceremos Wines and Spirits, 19 New Street, Horsforth, Leeds. Tel: 0113 205 4545. <www.vinceremos.co.uk>. UK's longest established organic wine specialist, plus beers, ciders, juices and spirits.

Vintage Roots, Farley Farms, Bridge Farm, Reading Road, Arborfield RG2 9HT. Tel: 0118 976 1999. <info@vintageroots.co.uk> <www.vintageroots.co.uk>. Huge range of organic wines, beers, ciders etc from around the world.

Chapter 7: Nitty-Gritty Eco-Living

Webwatch
Use it Again <www.useitagain.org.uk> (the official government recycling site)
Community Recycling Network: <www.crn.org.uk>
National Recycling Forum: <www.nrf.org.uk>

Bradford Waste Chasers Ltd, The Old Iron Mill, Lessarna Court, Bowling Back Lane, Bradford BD4 8ST. Tel/fax: 01274 720 740. Not-for-profit, co-operative company to promote waste reduction and recycling in West Yorkshire.

British Cycling Federation, Tel: 0161 230 2301. <www.bcf.uk.com>.

The Council for the Preservation of Rural England, 25 Buckingham Palace Road, London SW1W. Tel: 020 796 6433. <info@cpre.org.uk>.

Cyclists Touring Club, Tel: 01483 417 217. <www.ctc.org.uk>

Environmental Transport Association, 10 Church Street, Weybridge, Surrey KT13 8RS. Ethical breakdown and cycling assistance. Organize UK Car-Free Day. Tel: 01932 828882. <members@eta.co.uk>. <www.eta.co.uk>.

Going for Green, Elizabeth House, The Pier, Wigan WN3 4EX. Tel: 01942 612621, Fax: 01942 824778. <gfg@dircon.co.uk> <www.useitagain.org.uk>. National Campaign.

GreenChoices, PO Box 31617, London SW2 4FF.
<info@greenchoices.org> <www.greenchoices.org/recycling.html>.
Comprehensive information website on all green issues.

National Recycling Forum, Ground Floor, Europa House,
13–17 Ironmonger Road, London EC1V 3QG. Tel: 020 7253 6266.
<www.nrf.org.uk>.

Pleiades, 3 West Hill, London SW18 1RB. Tel: 020 8870 2138,
Fax: 0208870 4840. National centre for electric bicycles.

Real Nappy Association, PO Box 3704, London SE26 4RX.
Tel: 020 8299 4519. <www.realnappy.com>.

Respro, Unit 107, The Foundry Annexe, 65 Glasshill Street,
London SE1 0QR. Tel: 020 7721 7300. <www.respro.com>.
Manufacturer and retailer of anti-pollution masks for cyclists.

Waste Watch, Europa House, Ground Floor, 13–17 Ironmonger Row,
London EClV 3QG. <www.wastewatch.org.uk>. Promotes action on
waste reduction & recycling. Find out how and where your office can
donate used toner cartridges and raise funds for a nominated charity.

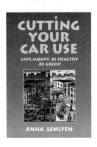

READING:
Cutting Your Car Use By Anna Semlyen (Green Books)

Also available from Green Books:

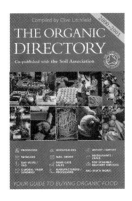

THE ORGANIC DIRECTORY
2000/2001 edition
Compiled & edited by Clive Litchfield

Includes • Retailers, producers, wholesalers and manufacturers of organic food • Vegetable box schemes (weekly boxes of in-season vegetables from organic farmers) • Local farmers' markets • Suppliers of organic gardening materials • Restaurants and accommodation specialising in organic food • and a wealth of other information. Published by Green Books with the Soil Association 192pp with index 234 x 156mm ISBN 1 870098 84 6 £7.95 pb

THE ORGANIC BABY & TODDLER COOKBOOK
Daphne Lambert and Tanyia Maxted-Frost

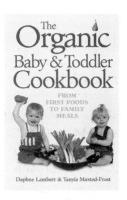

A comprehensive but easy-to-follow nutrition guide for babies from weaning to toddlerhood (four to six months to three years old). It includes the basic principles of good nutrition for mother and baby, information on why to eat organic (the positives and negatives in summary, with some statistics/facts thrown in for good measure), seasonal meal planners, recipes for meals and juices, tips on how to adapt the meals into the family routine, the ideal lunchbox, and more. Green Books 128pp ISBN 1 870098 86 2 £6.95 pb

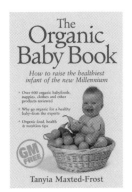

THE ORGANIC BABY BOOK
How to plan and raise a healthy child
Tanyia Maxted-Frost

The Organic Baby Book shows that it is now possible to eat, drink and buy nearly everything needed for mother and baby organically: fresh organic wholefoods • organic cotton reusable nappies (from seven companies) • ready-made babyfoods (over 11 brands) • cot blankets • bras and nursing pads • baby clothing • bodycare (over 30 brands) • food supplements • bedding • and more. Over 600 organic and environmentally-friendly products, companies, relevant organisations, annual events and useful resources are reviewed. Green Books 192pp 234 x 156mm ISBN 1 870098 79 X £7.95 pb

Also available from Green Books:

GENETIC ENGINEERING, FOOD, AND OUR ENVIRONMENT
A Brief Guide

Luke Anderson

This book aims to clarify some of the key issues that concern people about genetic engineering, and answer questions such as • What is genetic engineering? • Why are genetically engineered foods being introduced? • What are the implications for health, farming, and the environment? • Is genetic engineering needed to feed the growing world population? • Why are living organisms being patented? • Who is making the crucial decisions about the future of our food supply? • What can you do if you are concerned about these issues? Luke Anderson is a journalist, speaker and campaigner who specialises in issues related to genetic engineering. Green Books 160pp 177 x 122mm ISBN 1 870098 78 1 £3.95 pb

GAIA'S KITCHEN
Vegetarian Recipes for Family and Community from Schumacher College

Julia Ponsonby

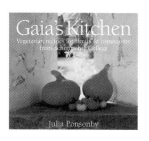

The cuisine at Schumacher College calls upon the best of Mediterranean, Californian, Indian, and Mexican vegetarian cooking, with old favourites rich in cheese and eggs, and also a variety of tempting new vegan dishes using ingredients such as pulses, tofu and tempeh. At the same time issues around food production, health and special diets are presented so that people can evolve a healthy diet, together with an awareness of ecological issues which affect our food today. Includes a full repertoire of menus: main courses, salads, soups, desserts, breads, cakes and biscuits; and gives community-size quantities as well as family-size quantities. Green Books 192 pages with colour and b&w photos 228 x 244mm ISBN 1 870098 93 5 £12.95 pb

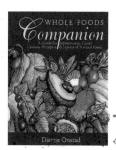

WHOLEFOODS COMPANION
Dianne L. Onstad

Includes detailed entries on hundreds of fruits, vegetables, grains, legumes, herbs and spices, nuts, seeds and oils; how to shop for, prepare, store and preserve whole foods; precise nutritional specifications, and an extraordinary depth of information on the beneficial health effects of eating wholefoods. Chelsea Green (USA) 400pp with 100 illus., 360 nutritional tables, bibliog. & index 250 x 195mm ISBN 0 930031 83 0 £19.95 pb

For our latest catalogue, phone 01803 863260
or visit our website at <www.greenbooks.co.uk>